YORK NOTES

General Editors: Professor A.N. Jeffares (University of Stirling) & Professor Suheil Bushrui (University of Beirut)

H.G. Wells
THE WAR OF THE WORLDS

Notes by Patrick Parrinder
BA PH D (CAMBRIDGE)
Lecturer in English, University of Reading

LONGMAN
YORK PRESS

YORK PRESS
Immeuble Esseily, Place Riad Solh, Beirut.

LONGMAN GROUP LIMITED
Burnt Mill,
Harlow, Essex

© Librairie du Liban 1981

All rights reserved. No part of this publication may be reproduced,
stored in a retrieval system, or transmitted in any form or by any
means, electronic, mechanical, photocopying, recording, or otherwise,
without the prior permission of the copyright owner.

First published 1981
ISBN 0 582 78134 5
Printed in Hong Kong by
Sheck Wah Tong Printing Press Ltd

Contents

Part 1: Introduction — page 5
  Wells's early life — 5
  The Theory of Evolution — 6
  Wells's career as a writer — 7
  Wells as a political thinker — 9
  Wells's imaginative characteristics — 10
  Science fiction — 11
  Is there life on Mars? — 12
  A note on the text — 13

Part 2: Summaries — 14
  A general summary — 14
  Detailed summaries — 16

Part 3: Commentary — 38
  The starting-point: what would happen if . . .? — 38
  The handling of the narrative — 39
  Style — 40
  Plot — 42
  The portrayal of the Martians — 44
  The response to the invasion — 47
  General themes and ideas: the 'dethronement of Man' — 51
  The ending of *The War of the Worlds* — 53
  Popularity and influence — 54

Part 4: Hints for study — 55
  Points to select for detailed study — 55
  Selection of key quotations — 57
  Specimen answers — 58
  Specimen questions — 61

Part 5: Suggestions for further reading — 63

The author of these notes — 64

Part 1
Introduction

Wells's early life

Herbert George Wells was born in 1866 at Bromley in Kent, a small town just outside London. His father was a shopkeeper and his mother had been a lady's maid. Wells was very conscious of his class origins, and when he became a world-famous writer he would frequently stress that he remained a 'common man', one of the ordinary people. In fact, the family was poor but intensely respectable. His mother was a devout Christian and tried hard to instil this faith in her children. Wells was sent to a private school for the sons of shopkeepers and businessmen and was encouraged not to mix with working-class children. In his own words, 'So far as the masses went I was entirely of my mother's way of thinking; I was middle-class,—"petty bourgeois" as the Marxists have it.'

No sooner had he begun to distinguish himself at school, however, than the family circumstances changed drastically. His father, never a very successful businessman, neglected the family shop until it went bankrupt. His mother went back to work as a resident housekeeper at a large country house, and Wells, like his brothers, was apprenticed to the drapery trade. As a shop assistant in a large store selling curtain fabrics, furniture coverings and dress materials, he was required to work for thirteen hours a day and to sleep in the communal dormitory above the shop. The apprentices, young boys who were bound to one employer while learning the trade, were allowed one and a half hour's free time in the evening before being locked in for the night. Wells worked in the drapery business for two years, between the ages of fourteen and sixteen. The experience left a very deep impression on a boy already becoming conscious of his exceptional intelligence and imaginative gifts. It was to become the basis of his two comic novels *Kipps* (1905) and *The History of Mr Polly* (1910).

In the end, Wells pleaded with his mother to let him leave the drapery trade, threatening to commit suicide if she would not listen. With the small amount of money she had saved she was able to repay the cost of his apprenticeship and to send him to the local Grammar School. After a year back at school he was awarded a government scholarship to train as a science teacher at the Normal School of Science (now

Imperial College, part of London University) in South Kensington. He entered the college as a biology student in the autumn of 1884.

Scientific education did not become widespread in Britain until the end of the nineteenth century, and Wells was one of the first generation of science students. He began studying biology shortly after the great public controversy over Charles Darwin's theory of Evolution, and his first teacher was Thomas Henry Huxley (1825–95), one of the most eminent of Victorian scientists. Although the two had little personal contact, Huxley's influence on the intellect and imagination of the young Wells was enormous. Many details in his books, including the opening sentence of *The War of the Worlds* with its reference to the view through a microscope, bear witness to Wells's fascination with biological study. Huxley, a philosopher and propagandist for science as well as a distinguished researcher, was both the friend of Darwin and the principal public champion of the theory of Evolution in its battle with orthodox religious opinion.

The Theory of Evolution

In the year 1800 orthodox Christians still believed in the literal truth of the creation story as told in the Bible. Scientific knowledge of the richness and diversity of the natural world was seen as an aid to the worship of God the Creator. Many of the early scientists were deeply religious men. To their growing dismay, the study of geology produced evidence which contradicted the Biblical assertion that the Earth was created in six days. The stratification of rocks and the location of fossil deposits led to the calculation that the age of the Earth must be measured in millions of years. Human life, and indeed all organic life, occupied no more than a tiny portion of this time-span.

In zoology, meanwhile, the classification of living species showed that Man, far from being specially created in the likeness of God, was a mammal closely allied to the apes. During the nineteenth century, several theories were put forward to explain the development of the different animal species, and to show how this development fitted in with geological discoveries. The theory that Darwin put forward in his book *The Origin of Species* (1859) came to be almost universally accepted by scientists. It has been repeatedly confirmed by more recent discoveries, especially in the field of genetics (the study of the variation of inherited characteristics from generation to generation).

According to Darwin, evolution takes place as a result of *natural selection*. Animal life is a 'struggle for existence', because far more members of any species are born than can find the means to survive. Within any species there is constant individual variation, and, in the competition for the means of subsistence, those individuals and varieties tend to survive which are best adapted to their environment. Since Darwin's death, the mechanism of variation or mutation within species has been fully explained by geneticists.

From the point of view of the species, animal reproduction may be viewed as an experimental process, aimed not only at replacing one generation by another, but at producing new individuals who may be better adapted to their environment than their predecessors. Often, however, the environment changes so drastically that the mechanism of natural selection cannot keep up with it. In that case the species dwindles or becomes extinct. A vast number of species have become extinct on Earth; the most spectacular of these, for us today as well as for their nineteenth-century discoverers, are the giant dinosaurs. The living species of our own epoch are the survivors of this long process of successive development and extinction. The main feature of the present stage of evolution is, of course, the dominance of Man over all other animals. Will his dominance continue, or are the forces already at work to bring about man's extinction? This question, which Wells first asked himself as a biology student, is basic in *The War of the Worlds*.

Wells's career as a writer

Wells's three years as a student (1884–7) were one of the most formative periods of his life. After finishing his biology course he went on to study physics and geology, but he lost interest in these subjects and devoted much of his time to literature and politics. He edited the college magazine, spoke in college debates and attended the meetings of the socialist movement which was emerging in Britain in the 1880s. (Wells would always remain close to the socialist movement, although bitterly critical of Marxism which he believed to be based on class hatred.) His neglect of his studies was such that he failed his final examination in 1887, and had to take up a teaching post in a private school. After a few months he was badly injured in a football accident, losing the use of a lung. The doctors did not expect him to survive, and his intellectual career seemed to be at an end.

Bed-ridden for several months, Wells at last found an opportunity to begin writing fiction. While recovering from his accident he began work on a realistic novel, attempting a life-like description of people in contemporary society. At the same time, he drew upon his scientific training to write the first of his fantastic stories concerned with the future. Called 'The Chronic Argonauts', it was published in the *Science Schools Journal* during 1888; after many revisions it was to become one of his finest works, *The Time Machine*. When his health had improved, Wells took up science teaching and also studied for the degree of B.Sc., which he gained in 1890. He wrote text-books and educational journalism and became, for a brief period, a literary and theatre critic. But all the time he was waiting for the opportunity to establish himself as a novelist and short-story writer. The moment came with the success of *The Time Machine* in 1895. During the years immediately after 1895 he published virtually all of his best science fiction, including three volumes of short stories and the novels *The Island of Dr Moreau* (1896), *The Invisible Man* (1897), *The War of the Worlds* (1898), *When the Sleeper Wakes* (1899) and *The First Men in the Moon* (1901).

After 1900 Wells embarked on his long series of realistic novels, drawing heavily on his own experiences and giving an incisive commentary on contemporary British society and manners. The best of these novels are *Tono-Bungay* (1909) and, in a more comic vein, *The History of Mr Polly* (1910); others, such as *Ann Veronica* (1909) and *The New Machiavelli* (1911), created a great deal of controversy at the time of publication because of their outspokenness about sexual relationships and their recognition of women's demand for equality. Wells himself after a brief, unhappy marriage to his cousin Isabel in the early 1890s, eloped with Amy Catherine Robbins, by whom he later had two sons. His second marriage was a stable one, but his continuing search for sexual fulfilment provided the impetus for the arguments in many of his later books in favour of 'free' relationships and mutual toleration.

At the same time as he was establishing himself as a novelist, Wells became increasingly influential as a thinker. *Anticipations* (1901) was the first of several books in which he tried to predict the social and technological developments of the twentieth century. (His technological predictions include the tank, aerial bombing and nuclear warfare, all of which he had described before the war of 1914–18.) Wells's vision of a rational world in which poverty, oppression and war would have been eliminated appears in *A Modern Utopia* (1905) and in many later books. His belief in a world revolution which would give scientists the power to construct the future of Man made him, in his own lifetime, one of the most widely read of twentieth-century prophets. His fame was such that in 1934 he was able to visit Stalin in the Kremlin and Roosevelt in the White House—and to publish his conversations with these two world leaders. In the same year he brought out his *Experiment in Autobiography*, which remains a masterly summary of his life and thought. He remained a very prolific writer throughout his life, being the author of over a hundred and fifty books and pamphlets. Unfortunately, many of his later works were hasty and repetitive tracts which added little to his overall reputation. Near the end of his life, Wells became increasingly subject to moods of despair, in which he took the Second World War as evidence of humanity's imminent self-destruction. He died in London on 13 August 1946, just a year after the atom-bombing of Hiroshima and Nagasaki. The nuclear age which he had prophesied in *The World Set Free* (1914) had come to pass, and his warnings, it seemed, had gone unheeded.

Wells as a political thinker

Trained as a scientist, Wells believed that the overriding problem of human life was that of *species survival*. In the peaceful late Victorian England in which he wrote *The War of the Worlds*, he was one of the few people to realise the vast destructive power of modern technology. The main threat to peace, as he saw it, was the economic and military rivalry of the advanced industrial nations. Towards the end of the First World War he became a keen supporter of the League of Nations movement, but was quickly disillusioned as it became clear that the League was powerless to override the autonomy of nation-states. In the late 1930s Wells was a member of the Sankey Committee on the Rights of Man, whose work anticipated the declaration of human rights in the United Nations charter. Wells believed that social problems must be tackled in the interest of the species as a whole, not of any particular class, nation or race. He put forward the idea of a world government, but believed that this could only come about by revolutionary means, as existing power-blocs and political leaders would never agree to it. He also warned repeatedly of the catastrophes to come if international co-operation was not achieved. Political problems, for Wells, were connected to a wider range of problems which he called those of 'human ecology'—the adaptation of the human species to its environment.

Wells began his working life as a schoolteacher, and his later work emphasises the need for education to form social values. As a critic of religion, imperialism and the nation-state, he noted how the narrowest and least progressive aspects of these institutions were propagated in the schools. His *Outline of History* (1920), one of his best-selling books, was an attempt to write a history of Mankind undistorted by national bias; it was succeeded by the much briefer *Short History of the World* (1922). Although these books were written long after his early science fiction, Wells's political and educational views are already hinted at in the Epilogue to *The War of the Worlds*, where he speaks of the benefits that the Martian invasion may have brought to Man. The 'conception of the commonweal of mankind' of which he speaks there was to become central to his political thought.

By the 'commonweal of mankind', Wells meant the socialist dream of a world united in its dedication to the brotherhood of Man. In many of his later books he discussed the practical means by which world unity could be brought about. His specific proposals for scientific and cultural co-operation, and for joint action to prevent the outbreak of war, anticipate the work of the United Nations today. Wells, however, believed in a much higher degree of world unification than has yet been achieved, and if he were alive today he would be bitterly disappointed at the way in which self-interest and the will of a few powerful nations and classes continues to dominate international politics.

Wells's imaginative characteristics

If Wells's intellect directed him towards science and politics, his creative temperament was by turns that of a visionary, a comic novelist in the Dickens tradition and a journalist. Prodigiously energetic, versatile, and never renowned for his capacity for patience, he wrote in a variety of literary forms without ever reaching the very highest level of literary achievement. That was his own opinion, and by and large most critics would agree with it. The exception is in the field of science fiction. But although it is as a science-fiction writer that Wells's reputation stands highest today, it should be remembered that he himself never valued this branch of his work as highly as his critics. Certainly he never surpassed his earliest works in this field, such as *The Time Machine* and *The War of the Worlds*.

In later life Wells accepted that he had not measured up to the high standards of artistic discipline set by other modern writers such as Joseph Conrad, Henry James and James Joyce, and concluded that he was not a 'novelist', in their refined sense, at all. In his realistic fiction he had used the novel as a vehicle for the discussion of ideas, for the analysis of patterns of human behaviour and for the portrayal of strictly contemporary social trends. His habit of introducing characters recognisably based upon well-known people into his later novels gives an idea of the topicality at which he aimed. Earlier on, however, Wells had shown many of the gifts of a social novelist in the nineteenth-century tradition, seeming to be an heir to Balzac and Dickens. His eye for the telling detail, his ear for the peculiarities of English speech and his irrepressible sense of fun all contribute to the enjoyment of a comedy such as *The History of Mr Polly*. But the quality of Wells's perceptions was often lost in the careless haste with which many of his later novels were written.

In his early science fiction novels such as *The War of the Worlds*, Wells is not a comic writer but a visionary and 'prophet'. On the surface these novels contain plenty of action and exciting events, but at the same time we are made aware of the seriousness of their concern with Man's ultimate destiny and the possibility that his enjoyment of power over nature will be short-lived. There were, in fact, two sharply different images of Man's future which influenced Wells in the 1880s and 1890s. The first was the *optimistic* vision of the utopian socialists, who looked forward to a perfected communist society in which scarcity and oppression would have been banished, and men would live free and untroubled lives. The second was the *pessimistic* vision of scientists such as T. H. Huxley, who believed that the long-term cooling of the Earth and the unpredictability of the process of evolution meant that civilisation could be maintained, if at all, only by constant vigilance and struggle against the changing environment. In his early science fiction Wells's vivid imagination inclined towards the second, pessimistic view. For example, the defeat of the Martians in *The War of the Worlds* is apparently a victory for humanity. But the victory is evidence not of man's strength but of his present weakness in the evolutionary struggle. In this book, as in much of his early science fiction, we are aware of the ironic quality of Wells's imagination rather than of his optimism.

Science fiction

Wells was perhaps the greatest pioneer of modern science fiction, a literary form of increasing significance in all industrialised countries. Drawing on various earlier literary traditions, his work brought together the typical elements of modern science fiction as no previous writer had done. (However, he himself did not use the term 'science fiction', but called his early fiction 'fantasies' or 'scientific romances'.)

Among the literary traditions upon which Wells drew, the following may be mentioned: (1) the *extraordinary* or *marvellous voyage*, going back to Homer's *Odyssey* and including such imaginative fictions of sea-voyages and shipwrecks as Defoe's *Robinson Crusoe* (1719), Poe's *Narrative of Arthur Gordon Pym* (1838) and Melville's *Moby Dick* (1851); (2) the *Utopia* or portrayal of an ideal State, such as Plato's *Republic*, More's *Utopia* (1516) and Bacon's *New Atlantis* (1626); (3) the eighteenth-century *conte philosophique* ('philosophical tale'), usually a satirical account of a journey through unfamiliar lands, such as Swift's *Gulliver's Travels* (1726) and Voltaire's *Candide* (1759); (4) the *Gothic novel* of horror and fantasy, and especially Mary Shelley's *Frankenstein* (1818), in which the horror results from a scientist's all-too-successful attempt to construct a living creature in the laboratory; and (5) the *catastrophe novel*, a realistic narrative of social disaster, including Defoe's *Journal of the Plague Year* (1722) and 'future war' stories such as Sir George Chesney's *The Battle of Dorking* (1871).

Wells's immediate predecessor in science fiction was the French writer Jules Verne (1828–1905). Verne was a writer of 'marvellous voyages' to the moon and to the unexplored parts of the Earth such as the ocean-bed, the subterranean regions and the polar ice-caps. He described these regions in accordance with contemporary scientific knowledge, and transported his characters there by means of new machines such as the submarine and the space rocket. Like Verne, Wells wrote adventure stories, but his stories were not based on foreseeable developments in exploration and technology, but on the more speculative treatment of scientific ideas and hypotheses. Wells's combination of a broadly philosophical interest with a deliberate application of scientific ideas is his main contribution to science fiction.

The War of the Worlds was written at a time of intense speculation about the possibility of life on the planet Mars (see the following section). In planning the novel, Wells asked himself the question: 'If there were intelligent beings on Mars, what would they be like?' The known scientific facts pointed to three conclusions: (1) the Martians need not be anything like human beings; (2) they would have had a longer history, and might therefore be more highly developed than men; and (3) they might be driven by the increasingly hostile Martian climate to seek to move to a warmer planet, such as the Earth. Wells's use of logical, deductive speculation of this kind as the foundation of his story has been adopted as a basic principle of much modern science fiction.

His range of science-fictional themes and plots has also been deeply influential. The 'war of the worlds' theme of conflict between earthmen and monstrous extra-terrestrial invaders has proved to be one of the most popular of all. Hundreds of imitations, adaptations and reworkings of this theme in prose fiction, films, television, radio and comic strips have made it into one of the stereotypes or mass-produced themes of science fiction. Few of these commercial adaptations contain a fraction of the imagination and care that Wells put into his book.

Is there life on Mars?

Wells draws on two main areas of scientific knowledge in *The War of the Worlds*. The first is biology (see section on 'The Theory of Evolution' above). The second is astronomy. In the course of the opening paragraphs of Book I, Chapter 1 Wells gives most of the scientific facts about Mars which are relevant to his story.

Mars is traditionally the star of war, and hence the most appropriate source for an invasion of the Earth. As the nearest planet to the Earth, it has always been of paramount interest to astronomers. One of the first scientists to study Mars systematically was the great Johannes Kepler (1571-1630). In some editions of *The War of the Worlds* the following quotation from Kepler's letter to Galileo appears as an epigraph on the title-page:

> But who shall dwell in these worlds if they be inhabited? ... Are we or they Lords of the World? ... And how are all things made for Man?

Kepler drew no conclusions as to the existence of life on other planets.

Speculation on this subject did not become widespread until the late nineteenth century, when the discoveries of G. V. Schiaparelli (1835–1910) and Percival Lowell (1855–1916) caused great popular excitement. It was Schiaparelli who in 1877 detected the markings on the surface of Mars which quickly became known as 'canals'. His researches established the topography of the planet with far greater precision than before. In 1894 Lowell founded an observatory at Flagstaff, Arizona, USA, specially devoted to the study of Mars, and two years later, in his book *Mars*, he announced his conviction that the network of 'canals' must be the artificial handiwork of intelligent Martians. Lowell argued that the canals must have been built for the purpose of irrigating the parched soil of the rapidly drying planet.

In the 1890s, therefore, there seemed to be very good reasons for suspecting the existence of life on Mars. Wells is known to have argued the case for the habitability of Mars during a college debate in 1888. Then in 1894 reports appeared in the scientific press of an intense glow of light on the surface of the planet. Some writers speculated that the Martians might be signalling to the Earth; the sober scientific journal *Nature*, on the other hand, suggested that the light could be caused by an enormous forest fire. Wells followed the reports and subsequent discussion closely, and his decision to write a novel on the highly topical subject of 'life on Mars' must have been taken soon afterwards.

Modern space exploration has shown almost conclusively that intelligent Martians do not exist and never have existed. But this is no obstacle to the continued enjoyment of Wells's fantasy.

A note on the text

The War of the Worlds was published in book form in January 1898, after serialisation in a popular fiction magazine, *Pearson's Magazine*, in 1897. It was included in Volume Three of the *Atlantic Edition of the Works of H. G. Wells*, with a new preface by the author, and in *The Scientific Romances of H. G. Wells* in 1933. The book has been translated into many languages. Shortly after its first appearance, a pirated American edition of the story showed the Martians landing near Boston, Massachusetts. In 1938 an American adaptation of *The War of the Worlds* for radio, read by Orson Welles, was so lifelike that it caused a nation-wide panic. In the 1953 Hollywood film version, directed by Byron Haskin, the Martians landed in Los Angeles. *The War of the Worlds* has been in print ever since its publication, and there are many adequate modern reprints based on the text of the first edition. However, the 'critical edition' edited by Frank D. McConnell, Oxford University Press, New York, 1977, reproduces a slightly abridged text.

Part 2

Summaries
of THE WAR OF THE WORLDS

A general summary

The Martian invasion took place at the beginning of the twentieth century. Ten spaceships or 'cylinders' were launched against the Earth, landing in a small area of South-East England. The Martian invaders attacked the spectators surrounding their first ship with the Heat-Ray, and advanced on London, killing and destroying wherever they went. Human weapons were no match for the enemy, and in a few days the social structure of Britain began to collapse. The narrator of the story, whose house was close to where the first cylinder landed, tells of his adventures as he flees before the Martians. He is trapped in a ruined house next to one of their encampments, and gets a closer view of the invaders and their technology than any other survivor of the battle. Meanwhile, his brother joins in the panic flight of refugees from London, and manages to escape overseas. After several days, the narrator escapes from his imprisonment in the ruined house, to find that London is deserted. Eventually he comes upon the bodies of the dead and dying Martians, who have been defeated, not by men, but by a mysterious, unseen enemy. The explanation of their defeat is a simple biological one. After the Martian collapse, the destruction they have caused is repaired, and the narrator is reunited unexpectedly with his wife.

The setting of *The War of the Worlds* is South-East England in the early years of the twentieth century. Wells gives a vividly accurate description of this part of England as he knew it when writing the story in the mid-1890s. At that time Queen Victoria was still on the throne and Great Britain was the world's most powerful country. The British Army and Navy had not been tested in a major war for many years. Wells shows that the British, accustomed to security, steady progress and commercial prosperity, have grown complacent, and that the shock of the Martian invasion is overwhelming.

The place names in the story are all real. The principal towns and villages mentioned are shown in the two maps on page 15 opposite. Map 1 shows South-East England as a whole; Map 2 shows the area between Woking in Surrey, where the narrator lives, and London. With the aid of Map 2 the reader may follow the Martians' progress from their first landing to the destruction of Weybridge and Shepperton (Book I, Chapter 12) and their advance on London.

Summaries · 15

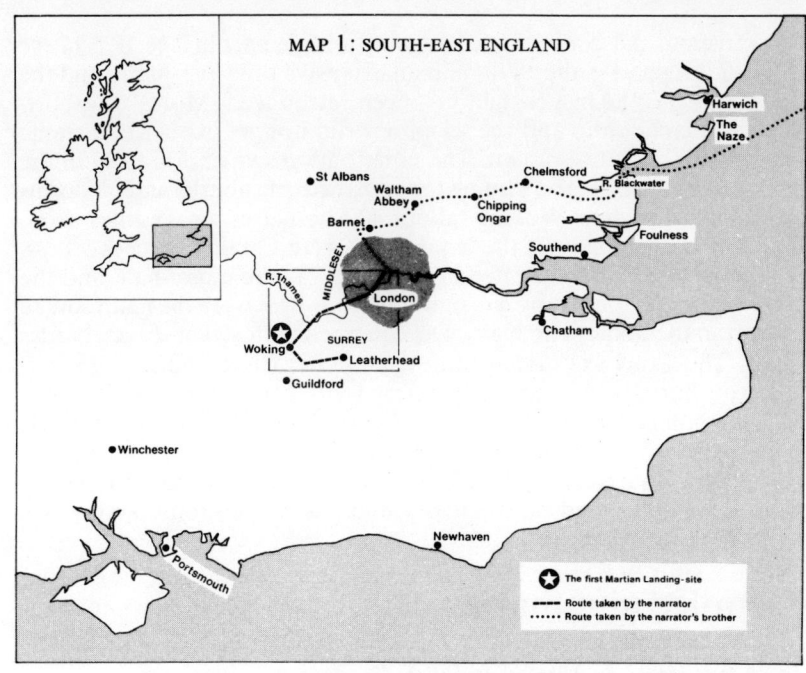

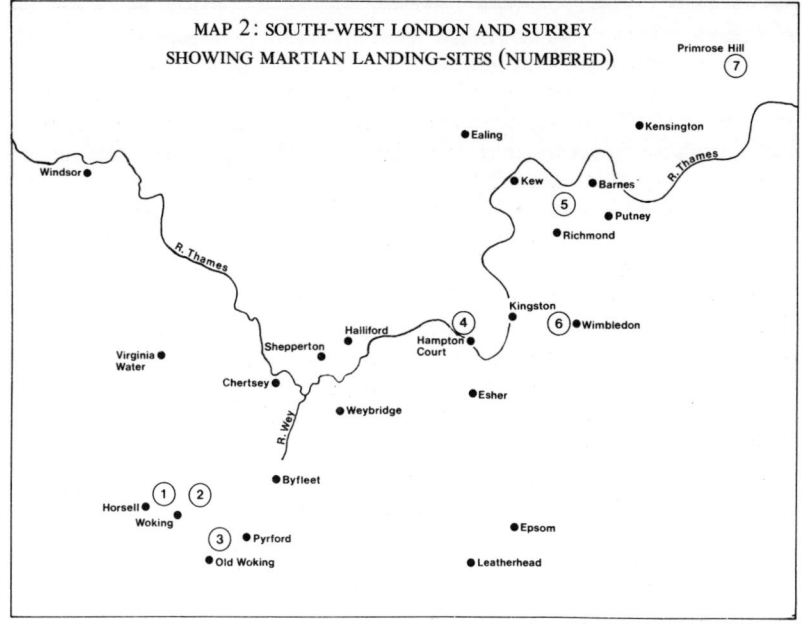

Transport and communications play a large part in *The War of the Worlds*. England in the 1890s had an extensive railway system, and the telegraph and the bicycle had just been introduced. Motor transport, the aeroplane, radio and the telephone did not yet exist. Road traffic was invariably horse-drawn. The cities had grown enormously in the previous hundred years, leading to the growth of suburbs and of 'dormitory towns' such as Woking (about 40 kilometres, or 25 miles, from London) where many of the inhabitants were London office-workers. The most popular form of entertainment was the music-hall, and the streets were lit at night by gas-lighting. Coal-fires were the main source of heat in the home. The Navy was equipped with steam-driven battleships. The Army was divided into the infantry (foot-soldiers), the cavalry (on horse-back) and the artillery (with horse-drawn field guns).

The book is dedicated to Frank Wells, H. G. Wells's elder brother, who suggested the idea of beings from another planet dropping suddenly out of the sky into the peaceful countryside around Woking. H. G. Wells and his second wife rented a house at the bottom of Maybury Hill, Woking in 1895–6.

Detailed summaries

Book I, Chapter 1: The Eve of the War

No one in the last years of the nineteenth century would have believed that intelligent beings somewhere in the universe were watching the affairs of men, let alone that the inhabitants of Mars were planning to invade the Earth. The atmosphere of Mars is capable of supporting life, but the planet is cooler than the Earth. The Martians are anxious to move to a warmer, more fertile world closer to the sun, and they are preparing to do battle with the inhabitants of Earth, whom they regard as inferior creatures to be ruthlessly destroyed.

The narrator, an Englishman, tells of a great light that was seen on Mars in 1894, probably caused by the casting of a huge gun. Some years later astronomers observe a series of ten explosions of flaming gas on the planet. These explosions are caused by the launching of the Martian invasion. Despite newspaper reports of the explosions, men go about their business and pleasure as if nothing had happened. Meanwhile, the Martian missiles are drawing near.

COMMENTARY: This chapter is packed with information necessary for the understanding of the story. Some of its themes are as follows:

1. the idea that Man is being watched by extra-terrestrial beings;
2. the development of life on Mars (see sections on 'The Theory of Evolution' and 'Is There Life on Mars?' in the Introduction);

3. the comparison of the Martians' attack on humanity with the behaviour of Europeans towards (*a*) extinct and near-extinct animals such as the bison and dodo, (*b*) primitive peoples such as the Tasmanians;
4. Man's inability to realise that he is in imminent danger.

NOTES AND GLOSSARY:
infusoria: a class of single-celled living organisms, visible only under the microscope
nebular hypothesis: the theory which supposes a nebula, or luminous cloud of gaseous matter, to be the original state of the solar system. As cooling took place, the nebula condensed into first a liquid and then a solid state, to form the sun. The planets were formed as a result of matter breaking away from the sun. The process of cooling on each planet is irreversible but, at the surface of the planet, such cooling is 'secular', or in other words very long periods of extreme cold are followed by equally long periods of comparative warmth ('Ice Ages' and temperate ages). Wells describes Mars in the grip of a new Ice Age
lemur: a nocturnal animal allied to the monkeys
the vanished bison and the dodo: the bison or wild ox once roamed the plains of Europe and North America. The vast herds of North American bison were hunted almost to extinction in the mid-nineteenth century. The dodo, an extinct flightless bird, was discovered by Portuguese sailors on the island of Mauritius in 1507. Persecuted by Man and the animals he introduced into the island, it had vanished by 1681
the Tasmanians: the extinct population of Tasmania, a large island to the south of Australia. Wells refers to the Black War, waged against the Tasmanians by European settlers from 1804 onwards. The last native Tasmanian died in South Australia in 1888
the opposition of 1894: a planet is in opposition when the Earth lies directly between it and the sun. Since the whole sunward side of the planet is turned towards the Earth, this affords the best conditions for astronomical observation
the issue of *Nature* dated August 2: the report that Wells mentions actually appeared in *Nature*, a weekly scientific journal. The Lick Observatory is in California, U.S.A. J.A. Perrotin was the director of the Nice Observatory in France, but the name of his assistant, Javelle, has been changed by Wells to 'Lavelle of Java'

the astronomical exchange: an arrangement for circulating astronomical information by telegraph
spectroscope: an instrument of chemical analysis, which examines the refraction of a beam of light through the substance to be analysed
Punch: in the nineteenth century the political cartoon was one of the best-known features of this weekly humorous magazine
For my own part ... progressed: the activities described in this sentence were those of H. G. Wells himself, when he lived at Woking in the year 1895-6

Book I, Chapter 2: The Falling Star

The first of the Martian missiles lands on Horsell Common. It is discovered by Ogilvy, the astronomer, who believes it to be a meteorite. The missile is cylindrical in shape, and Ogilvy perceives that its top is slowly rotating. He concludes that there are men trapped inside it, but the cylinder is too hot to approach, so he runs to fetch help. Henderson, a journalist, goes with him to inspect the cylinder, and sends news of its landing to London. Meanwhile, the narrator hears the (by now considerably distorted) news of the cylinder's arrival, and goes to the Common to see for himself.

COMMENTARY: This chapter describes the experiences of Ogilvy, the astronomer. As a qualified observer, it is he who realises that the 'meteorite' is connected with the flashes of light on Mars that were described in the previous chapter.

NOTES AND GLOSSARY:
meteorite: a ball of matter that has fallen out of the sky on to the Earth. Falling meteorites become extremely hot owing to the friction of the Earth's atmosphere
common: a large open space, belonging to the local community as a whole. Horsell Common is just outside Woking and contains trees, scrub and sand-pits
a huge cylinder: the Martian space-ships are referred to as 'cylinders' throughout the story
potman: a barman in a public-house or licensed drinking establishment

Book I, Chapter 3: On Horsell Common

The narrator arrives to find about twenty people gathered around the cylinder. The unscrewing of the top has ceased. The casual onlookers do not understand what they are seeing, but the narrator's trained scientific eye picks out the signs of the cylinder's extra-terrestrial origin. Meanwhile, the news of its landing spreads, and as the day goes on a large crowd gathers. Stent, the Astronomer Royal, arrives with a team of workmen, intending to dig out the part of the cylinder which is embedded in the ground. It is decided to move back the crowd in order to let the excavation proceed.

NOTES AND GLOSSARY:
loafers: idle spectators
gas-float: a gas-powered signalling device, shaped at the bottom like a ship
no common oxide: metals are converted to oxides by atmospheric corrosion. The Martian cylinder is presumably made from a metal not usually found on Earth
containing manuscript: containing a handwritten message
three kingdoms: England, Scotland and Wales
flys . . . basket chaise: small horse-drawn carriages
Astronomer Royal: the official title of the director of the national observatory of Great Britain (formerly situated at Greenwich)
lord of the Manor: the owner of a landed estate, in this case the land around Woking
Waterloo: the London terminus of the railway line to Woking

Book I, Chapter 4: The Cylinder Unscrews

The narrator returns to the Common at sunset. The top of the cylinder is being unscrewed again, and the crowd of onlookers has become dense and so over-excited that a young shop-assistant has fallen into the pit thrown up by the impact of the cylinder. The lid of the cylinder falls off, and the first of the Martians emerges. The shop-assistant, having failed to climb out of the pit, is seized by the Martians and disappears with a scream. The activities of the Martians are hidden from view by the sides of the pit, which the onlookers are now too scared to approach.

COMMENTARY: In this chapter we are given the first description of the Martians. They are repulsive, reptilian beings. The appearance of the Martians here should be compared with later descriptions, especially those in Book II, Chapter 2.

NOTES AND GLOSSARY:
Gorgon group of tentacles: The Gorgons of Greek mythology were three frightful maidens, whose hair was made up of hissing snakes
fungoid: resembling a fungus or mushroom

Book I, Chapter 5: The Heat-Ray

Their confidence gradually returning, the onlookers begin to move back towards the pit. A deputation of men waving a white flag approaches the Martians, as if to negotiate with them. Suddenly the Martians use the Heat-Ray to attack the deputation and the crowds of people on the Common. The Heat-Ray burns everything in its path, and it is only by good fortune that the narrator himself escapes being burnt to death. He runs from the Common in terror.

COMMENTARY: In this chapter the basic pattern of the war between Martians and men is set. As in many later episodes, the Martians attack and kill defenceless human beings with vastly superior force. Why do they attack so ruthlessly? Are they wicked or wrong to do so?

The narrator discusses how the Heat-Ray works at the beginning of the next chapter.

NOTES AND GLOSSARY:
a thin rod ... circular disc: the rotating Heat-Ray is mounted on a periscope device, which enables the Martians to burn up the surrounding Common and the people on it while themselves remaining hidden in the pit
knoll: a small hill
Deputation: a group of people undertaking a mission on behalf of others. The deputation of Ogilvy, Stent and Henderson consists of the most highly-educated and scientifically-trained of the spectators (apart from the narrator). The white flag is a sign of peace, which the Martians simply ignore

Book I, Chapter 6: The Heat-Ray in the Chobham Road

About forty people are killed by the operation of the Heat-Ray, and the scrub-fires started by it burn all night. A crowd of spectators approaching the Common are saved by the lucky intervention of a low sand-dune between the road and the pit. They feel the beam of the Heat-Ray passing close over their heads, and they are so panic-stricken that at least three people are trampled to death.

COMMENTARY: In contrast to the preceding chapters (3–5), which describe the narrator's own experiences, the chapter is pieced together by the narrator from the reports of other witnesses.

NOTES AND GLOSSARY:
slay men so swiftly and so silently: the principle of the Heat-Ray is that heat energy generated in a furnace is projected in a

beam reflected from a parabolic mirror. This must be done without the normal rapid energy-loss caused by conductivity and atmospheric absorption. The construction of a Heat-Ray represents a technical advance unattainable on Earth before the mid-twentieth century invention of the laser beam.

gloaming: dusk
hummock: a low hill

Book I, Chapter 7: How I Reached Home

The narrator describes how he reached home. Once he has left the Common he forgets his terror and finds it hard to believe the astonishing things he has seen. The ordinary people of Woking treat the tale of the Martian landings as a joke, although the narrator's wife takes it seriously. As he recovers from his ordeal, the narrator complacently reasons that the Martians must be physically helpless on Earth, and that, despite their aggressive actions, they can be easily dealt with.

COMMENTARY: In this chapter the narrator describes his own conflicting emotions as he looks back on the dramatic events of the day. Finally he compares himself to 'some respectable dodo in the Mauritius' facing extinction as a result of the arrival of the colonists.

NOTES AND GLOSSARY:
row of gables: a row of houses with gabled roofs
'Ain't yer just been there?': here, as elsewhere in the book, Wells uses phonetic spelling to indicate the working-class dialect of the Woking district (a variant of the Cockney, or London, dialect)
the gravitational difficulty: in Chapter 4 the narrator saw a Martian fall over the side of the cylinder into the pit. The Martians cannot move easily on Earth because of the difference in gravity. The narrator does not anticipate that the Martians (like today's astronauts) are equipped with specially-designed vehicles to overcome this difficulty
argon: an inert gas found in small quantities in the Earth's atmosphere
erethism: abnormal excitement

Book I, Chapter 8: Friday Night

The Martians' arrival at first causes little stir outside the immediate surroundings of Woking. The London papers judge Henderson's telegram to be a hoax. In the Woking area itself, life goes on almost unchanged. Some people venture out in the darkness towards the pit, and are killed by the Heat-Ray. The Martians are building their Fighting Machines, and the noise of hammering is heard from the pit. Companies of soldiers converge on the scene, and the second Martian cylinder lands nearby.

NOTES AND GLOSSARY:
dovetailing: merging
canard: a hoax or false report
trenching on Smith's monopoly: The firm of W.H. Smith and Son had the sole right to sell newspapers at railway stations such as Woking. The boy is an unauthorised seller 'trenching on' or infringing this right
Inkerman barracks: these were situated at Knaphill, near Woking
squadron of hussars: a detachment of light cavalry
Maxim: an early form of machine-gun

Book I, Chapter 9: The Fighting Begins

The lull in the Martians' activities continues. The narrator walks towards the Common, but is turned back by a company of soldiers. He tries to get news of the Martians, and the sight of the army preparing to resist the invasion excites him to a pitch of war fever. He hears firing in the distance, and then the Martians use the Heat-Ray again, turning it on Maybury Hill where he is now sitting at home with his wife. He decides to abandon his house at once, and borrows a horse and cart before the majority of his neighbours have realised their common danger. He and his wife escape with their most valuable belongings towards Leatherhead.

COMMENTARY: In this chapter Wells uses a variety of characters to express different attitudes towards the coming battle.

NOTES AND GLOSSARY:
chariot: milk-cart
sappers: private soldiers belonging to the Royal Engineers
Horse Guards: the army headquarters in Whitehall, London
fishers of men: a reference to Christ's words in the Bible (St. Matthew 4:19)
Oriental College: the Oriental Institute of Woking was the headquarters of the British Muslim Society. Attached to it was the Shah Jehan Mosque, built in 1889 and still in use today
Spotted Dog: the name of the public-house on Maybury Hill

dogcart: a type of small horse-drawn carriage
thing like a dish cover: this is the 'metal shield' used to cover the Martians' advance (see Chapter 11). It consists of a Fighting Machine in the prone rather than the erect position

Book I, Chapter 10: In the Storm

The narrator leaves his wife in safety at Leatherhead and returns toward Woking later the same night, intending to give back the horse and cart he has hired. He sees the third cylinder landing, and simultaneously a thunderstorm breaks out. His horse bolts, and two Martian Fighting Machines appear over the horizon, coming towards him. In his terror the narrator overturns the cart, while the huge Fighting Machine passes overhead. When it has gone, he continues on foot in the pouring rain, stumbling over the dead body of the man from whom he has hired the dog-cart, and eventually arriving back at his house.

COMMENTARY: Here the monstrous Fighting Machines of the Martians make their first appearance. The terrifying effect of their appearance is heightened by Wells's description of the thunderstorm and the bolting of the horse. The melodramatic use of a thunderstorm is a frequent device in nineteenth-century fiction. Here it adds to the confusion of the scene and to the sense of a monstrous disruption of the natural order.

NOTES AND GLOSSARY:
in monosyllables: in the shortest words possible (literally, in words of one syllable)
in at the death: present at the kill
tripod: a three-footed structure
College Arms: name of a public-house

Book I, Chapter 11: At the Window

The narrator recovers from his journey and surveys the scene from an upstairs window in his house. He sees the black shapes of the Martians in the pit, lit up by the glare from the burning countryside. A soldier, the survivor of an artillery regiment that has been wiped out by the Martians, comes into the garden. The narrator invites him indoors, and hears his story. They return to the window together, contemplating the wreckage of Woking and its surroundings until daybreak.

COMMENTARY: The keynote of this chapter is destruction. This is vividly expressed by means of the eye-witness report of a new character (the artilleryman), as well as the description of the scene from the narrator's window. After the thunderstorm of the last chapter, this chapter is dominated by images of fire and smoke.

NOTES AND GLOSSARY:
the Potteries: the industrial district around Stoke-on-Trent in the English Midlands. In his short story 'The Cone' (1897), Wells describes how this area was lit up at night by the fires of pottery kilns
colossi: gigantic statues
sluggish lumps: the octopus-like Martians
ironclad: an armour-plated battleship
unlimbered: prepared for action
Titan: the Titans were legendary Greek gods. The term is also used to describe machines of great size and power

Book I, Chapter 12: What I saw of the Destruction of Weybridge and Shepperton

In the morning the narrator and the artilleryman set off together to make their escape. A cavalry officer, met with on the road, orders the artilleryman to report to Weybridge, and the narrator guides him there. They pass further military detachments and observe the evacuation of civilians on the road. At Weybridge all is in confusion. They come down to the River Thames, and then firing is heard and five Martian Fighting Machines come into sight. The crowd of refugees panics, and the narrator and others plunge into the river, hoping to escape the Heat-Ray. Shells from a concealed gun-battery succeed in killing one of the Martians; the machine it is directing continues unaided, until it collapses into the river. Caught in the boiling water, the narrator watches the other Martians inspecting the remains of their dead comrade. Then, as the Martians return upstream, using their Heat-Rays indiscriminately, he crawls up onto the river-bank, escaping death by a miracle.

COMMENTARY: The war reaches its first climax, as the full strength of the Martians and the human defences are now pitted against one another. This is the longest and most eventful chapter so far. The narrator is in the thick of the action, as one sensational development follows another. Wells's description of a purely imaginary battle is, in fact, more vivid than many descriptions of real battles.

NOTES AND GLOSSARY:
battery: a small detachment of artillery
theodolite: an instrument used in land-surveying

heliograph:	an instrument for signalling by means of flashes of sunlight
'luminium:	aluminium
grenadiers:	members of the regiment of Grenadier Guards
prohibited hours:	hours at which public-houses are closed by law
pollard willows:	willow-trees which have been pruned back to the trunk
sojers:	soldiers (phonetic spelling)
tidal bore:	a huge wave
wheal:	a ridge
spit:	a bank of sand or gravel projecting into the water
a score of yards:	twenty yards

Book I, Chapter 13: How I fell in with the Curate

After the battle at Weybridge and Shepperton, the Martians withdraw to their base on Horsell Common. Both sides are engaged in preparations for the coming war. Meanwhile, the narrator makes his way down the river towards London. He finds an abandoned boat, and drifts for a while downstream. He lands on the river-bank and, exhausted, falls asleep. He wakes to find another man beside him—a Church of England curate who has been driven to the edge of insanity by the destruction of Weybridge. As they hear the guns begin firing again, the two men set off together in the direction of London.

COMMENTARY: The narrator's view of events is now contrasted with that of the curate, a religious fanatic who plays an important part in later chapters. The curate is blind to the real nature of the Martian invasion, believing it to be evidence of God intervening directly in the affairs of the Earth. His belief that the end of the world has come, though mistaken, reflects the magnitude of the disaster that has taken place.

NOTES AND GLOSSARY:
the earthquake that destroyed Lisbon a century ago: this famous earthquake took place in 1755. Within fifteen minutes two-thirds of the city had collapsed in ruins
parboiled: half-boiled
curate: a Church of England clergyman's assistant
mackerel sky: a sky dappled with small white fleecy clouds
Sodom and Gomorrah: in the Bible, two cities of Palestine destroyed by God as a punishment for the sins of their inhabitants
Sunday-schools: schools offering religious instruction on Sundays
The great and terrible day of the Lord: the second coming of Christ, as foretold in the Bible
cockchafer: a small flying insect

Book I, Chapter 14: In London

Chapters 14, 16 and 17 tell of the experiences of the narrator's younger brother, a medical student living in London.

Hearing of the Martians' landing, and believing that they pose little threat to humanity, the narrator's brother decides to travel down to Woking to see the creatures for himself. He arrives at Waterloo Station late on Saturday night to find that the railway line to Woking is closed, though nobody knows why. Despite the reports in the Sunday newspapers, next day London remains calm. The narrator's brother returns to Waterloo, and witnesses the passage of soldiers and guns. Reports of the fighting at Weybridge reach London, as do the first refugees from Surrey. The noise of firing is heard, and early on Monday morning the people of London are ordered to evacuate the city. The narrator's brother prepares to leave amid the growing panic.

COMMENTARY: Wells is obliged to introduce a new narrator in order to give an eye-witness report of developments in London. The aim of this chapter is to set the scene for Chapter 16, which describes the panic-stricken flight of London's six million inhabitants before the Martian invaders. The piecemeal way in which the news of the Martians spreads is particularly effective here.

NOTES AND GLOSSARY:
cab: a horse-drawn taxi
Referee: a Sunday newspaper
menagerie: a collection of wild animals
what the dickens: what! (emphatic)
'lungs': open spaces near a city
the South-Eastern and the South-Western stations: Waterloo Station is divided into two parts, which belonged to different railway companies
Salvation Army: a Christian evangelical organisation
quasi proclamation: a semi-official announcement
raiment: clothing
Sabbath-best: dressed for church-going
Derby Day: the day of the annual horse-race for the Derby Stakes
promenaders: people walking about for the sake of amusement
sheet lightning: lightning seen reflected through clouds
shilling: old unit of British money used before the introduction of decimal currency; a shilling was worth one-twentieth of a pound sterling
en masse: (*French*) in a mass
ejaculating: muttering prayers or curses

Book I, Chapter 15: What Had Happened in Surrey

After their withdrawal, the Martians come out again and resume the attack. One of the Fighting Machines is damaged by artillery fire, but the machine is repaired by the Martian who is operating it. As the enemy advance continues, the narrator and the curate observe another new weapon that each of the Martians possesses. This is a heavy tube or gun, firing shells containing a poisonous black gas. The Martians use this Black Smoke, rather than the Heat-Ray, to destroy the military units that are lying in wait for them. By dawn on Monday the Martians have entered the suburbs of London, with the population flying before them.

COMMENTARY: Wells's description of the effects of the Black Smoke may now be read as a prophetic anticipation of the effects produced by poison gas in the First World War, roughly twenty years after the book was written.

NOTES AND GLOSSARY:
ululation: a moaning or crying noise
blight: a disease in plants, caused by parasites
crescent: a figure in the shape of the old or new moon
powder-mills: factories for making explosives
a greater Moscow: in 1812 the city of Moscow was evacuated and burned to forestall the advance of Napoleon's army
minute-guns: guns firing at intervals of a minute
kopje: a small hill
carbonic acid gas: carbon dioxide (CO_2)
volcanic clefts: cracks in rock made by the action of a volcano
a group of four lines in the blue of the spectrum: a reference to spectroscopic analysis (see Notes to Book I, Chapter 1 on *spectroscope*)
quick-firers: machine-guns

Book I, Chapter 16: The Exodus from London

As the Martians approach the centre of their city, the people of London awake to the need for immediate flight. The roads and railways are soon crowded with panic-stricken people. The narrator's brother, having failed to fight his way aboard a train, takes part in the looting of a cycle shop, and makes his way northward on a damaged bicycle until it becomes unrideable. Once outside the city he starts walking eastward, with the idea of making for the coast. He comes upon three men who are attacking two ladies driving in a pony-carriage. He fights off the men, and accompanies the ladies in the carriage until they reach the

Great North Road, which they have to cross. On the road is a dense crowd of terrified refugees, pouring out of London. Many of the refugees are in a desperate condition, and among them is the Lord Chief Justice, who is at the point of death. Later a man is killed as he dives under a horse-driven cab to retrieve a bag of gold coins. Appalled by these sights, the narrator's brother wants to turn back, but he sees there is no alternative to crossing the stream of traffic. Helped by one of the ladies, he forces the cart out onto the highway. They are swept onward for a mile or so before they are able to turn off to the east. Finally they stop for the night, exhausted by the violence of the exodus from the city.

COMMENTARY: This dramatic chapter is a remarkable description of social collapse. At the beginning Wells uses the image of society turning from solid into liquid form, as if London itself is dissolving into tidal waves or torrents of people pouring out in every direction. The scene on the Great North Road shows such a torrent at close quarters. The fury and violence of this 'exodus from London' are in some ways reminiscent of medieval visions of Hell. The narrator's brother refers to the crowd on the road as 'hell', and some of the incidents he describes seem designed to illustrate the traditional 'Deadly Sins' of greed and rage. The tumultuous procession described in Percy Bysshe Shelley's poem 'The Triumph of Life' (1822) may also have been in Wells's mind as he wrote this chapter. The reader may like to consider whether in actuality the people of a large city would respond to the threat of invasion with the kind of panic that Wells describes.

NOTES AND GLOSSARY:
the South-Eastern people: the London and South-Eastern Railway
stile: a gate or step-ladder leading into a field
pugilistic chivalry: observance of the rules of boxing
rahnd: round (phonetic spelling)
gride: grating sound
host: crowd of people
bit: the mouthpiece of a horse's harness
Vestry: the governing body of a parish or small district
roughs: rough or uncultivated people
brewer's dray: a low cart for carrying beer-barrels
galvanized: stimulated
privet: a type of bush used for garden hedges

Book I, Chapter 17: The 'Thunder Child'

While the six million inhabitants of London are evacuating the city, the Martians go on with their terrible advance. Three more of their cylinders land in the London suburbs. Meanwhile, the Government, which has retreated to Birmingham, makes unsuccessful attempts to regain control of the people. The narrator's brother and his companions continue eastwards until they reach the coast, where boats of all kinds are taking on passengers who wish to fly across the North Sea. Some time after they have gone on board ship, three Martians appear on shore. The Martians wade into the sea after the boats, but they are intercepted by an armoured battleship, the *Thunder Child*. The *Thunder Child* drives straight at the Martian Fighting Machines, and destroys two of them before itself being blown up by the Heat-Ray. Under cover of the battle the refugee ships escape, leaving England behind in the twilight.

COMMENTARY: This is the second major battle-scene in the book. The first (Book I, Chapter 12) involved the army; this one involves the navy. The torpedo-ram proves the most effective of the various human weapons that are brought against the Martians, but only because of the recklessness with which its crew launch their surprise attack.

NOTES AND GLOSSARY:
stippled: covered with spots
Goths and Huns: tribes which invaded and devastated Europe during the third to fifth centuries AD
blotted: splashed, like ink-drops on paper
ham-stringing: destroying the activity of
Committee of Public Supply: probably an allusion to the Committee of Public Safety, the governing body of France during the Terror of 1793-4
fishing-smacks: small fishing-boats
colliers: coal-carrying ships
douche: shower of water
torpedo-ram: a battleship fitted with a battering-ram and with torpedo-tubes
leviathan: a giant sea-monster
starboard and larboard: the right- and left-hand sides of a ship respectively, from the point of view of a person facing toward the front of the ship

Book II, Chapter 1: Under Foot

Having told of his brother's escape from England, the narrator now returns to his own experiences. When the chapter opens he and the curate are hiding in an empty house at Halliford, surrounded by the Black Smoke. After two days a Martian appears, playing a jet of steam on the Smoke to disperse it. Determined to rejoin his wife if possible, the narrator leaves the house now that it is safe to do so, and the curate follows him. They go through Richmond to Kew, where they have two near escapes from the Martians, one of which is seen picking up human beings and tossing them into a metal basket carried behind it. The narrator and the curate struggle on after dark, and finally break into a house near Mortlake. They are eating food found in the kitchen when there is an explosion, and part of the house collapses. Eventually they realise that the house has been hit by the impact of the fifth Martian cylinder. They are trapped in the buried kitchen, while outside they can hear the noises of the Martians emerging from the cylinder and setting up the latest of their military bases.

COMMENTARY: The purpose of this chapter is to put the narrator in a position from which he can observe the behaviour of the Martians closely and accurately. At the same time, Wells introduces certain details which foreshadow later developments. The 'red masses' floating down the river are not corpses, as the narrator seems to think, but patches of the Red Weed. Also, the narrator sees a Martian collecting human beings and throwing them into the metallic 'basket' that was described in Book I, Chapter 10. What is he collecting them for?

NOTES AND GLOSSARY:
superheated: heated under pressure to a very high temperature
Pompeii: Roman city destroyed by the eruption of Mount Vesuvius in AD 79

Book II, Chapter 2: What We Saw from the Ruined House

The narrator and the curate take turns at looking through a hole in the wall which separates them from the Martian encampment. The kitchen in which they are hiding is perched on the edge of the huge pit dug by the cylinder. Within the pit, the narrator sees several of the Martians' machines. Among these are Fighting Machines and Handling Machines; the latter are used to erect the Fighting Machines. The Martians themselves are also seen in detail for the first time. Their bodies consist essentially of two parts, the head and the bunches of tentacles around the mouth which may be likened to hands. The Martians have no digestive organs, but live by injecting animal blood directly into their bloodstream. They have brought a few creatures resembling human beings from Mars to sustain them on the journey. The Martians need no sleep, and are not divided into sexes, but reproduce in the manner of vegetables and the lower organisms. They wear no clothing, and communicate directly by telepathic means, rather than by speech or gesture. Their technology is based on the imitation of the motions of animal muscles, and does not include the wheel. Finally, the narrator describes the operation of a Martian digging machine, which appears to be fully automatic.

COMMENTARY: This chapter, which should be studied with close attention, contains the most extensive descriptions of the Martians and their technology in *The War of the Worlds*. The narrator criticises an earlier 'hastily compiled pamphlet' on the invasion, and boasts that 'no surviving human being saw so much of the Martians in action as I did'. In addition to being an eye-witness account, the chapter has the air of a scientific paper detailing a series of observations of the Martians and drawing general conclusions from them. All in all, it is a very remarkable example of the use of the scientific imagination in literature.

NOTES AND GLOSSARY:
Handling Machines: the most remarkable aspect of these machines from an earthly point of view is the absence of the wheel and the axle from their design. Instead, they embody the principles of muscular action, and are constructed of a multitude of levers, bars and discs activated by electric currents. The technology of the Handling Machines was apparently imitated on Earth after the defeat of the Martian invasion
Dutch doll: a china doll
integument: skin or covering
tympanic surface: the surface of the ear-drum
Professor Howes: Professor T. G. B. Howes (1853–1905) taught zoology at the Normal School of Science (see p.5)
pulmonary distress: difficulty in breathing
pipette: a small pipe or tube
siliceous: containing the mineral silica
polyp: a general term for various types of marine organism
Tunicates: a class of marine animals characterised by a pouch-like body enclosed in a tough leathery skin
a certain speculative writer of quasi-scientific repute: the writer referred to humorously here was, in fact, Wells himself. His article 'The Man of the Year Million' had suggested that human evolution might be expected to proceed until all the present bodily organs had been made superfluous by the development of machinery, except for the brain and the hand. In a million years' time Man might consist of an enormous brain, a large pair of hands, and little else. If this prediction is taken seriously in the context of *The War of the Worlds*, the Martians become literally 'men of the future', who have reached their present state because life on Mars is considerably more advanced than on Earth, due to the greater distance of Mars from the sun

emotional substratum: the basis or foundation of the emotional life
carmine: a shade of red
suctional operation: the operation of sucking in blood
Lilienthal soaring-machines: Otto Lilienthal (b.1848) was a pioneer of aviation. He was killed when one of his craft crashed in flight in 1896
pivot: a shaft or axle forming the centre on which something turns
friction bearings: those parts of a machine which bear the friction caused by the moving parts

Book II, Chapter 3: The Days of Imprisonment

As their imprisonment continues, the relations between the narrator and the curate grow worse. The two quarrel and fight over the store of food in their hiding-place, and over the right to look through the peep-hole in the wall. A second Fighting Machine arrives in the pit, bringing an aluminium smelting device which is used to manufacture aluminium bars. Then some men are brought to the pit, and the Martians are seen feeding off human blood. In distress at this terrible sight, the narrator tries vainly to think of some plan of escape, while the curate gives way to blind terror. On the fourth or fifth night of their captivity, the sound of heavy guns is heard.

NOTES AND GLOSSARY:
oscillated: swung to and fro
spatulate: having a broadened and rounded end
clinkers: lumps of waste formed in the process of extracting metal from ore in a furnace

Book II, Chapter 4: The Death of the Curate

On the sixth day, the narrator finds the curate drinking in secret. He tries to divide the food into rations, but the curate has lost all self-control. Declaring that the invasion is a just punishment for man's sins, and shouting at the top of his voice, he prepares to give himself up to the Martians. Before he can do this, the narrator knocks him down with an axe. One of the Martians hears the noise, and puts its tentacle in through the hole in the wall. The narrator hides in the coal-cellar as the curate's body is dragged away. The Martian's tentacle comes back, and touches the narrator's boot as he lies hidden in the cellar. Finally, after a day of hiding, the narrator comes out into the kitchen to look for food and drink.

COMMENTARY: In this chapter the narrator is personally involved in violence. He acts ruthlessly in knocking down the curate, though this may be looked upon as a mistaken attempt to save him from the Martians. The narrator's contempt for the curate and his fanatical Christianity is made clear at several points in the story, however, and it would seem that he acted largely for reasons of self-preservation. His own defence of his actions is found in the third and fourth paragraphs of Book II, Chapter 3, and in the second paragraph of Book II, Chapter 7. But it is for the reader to decide how far the narrator's attack on the curate is justifiable.

NOTES AND GLOSSARY:
the wine-press of God and **the other voices of the trumpet:** phrases from the Bible. Both are taken from the Book of Revelation and refer to God's punishment of sinful mankind
Briareus: in Greek mythology, a hundred-handed giant

Book II, Chapter 5: The Stillness

Weak from hunger, the narrator discovers that all the food has been taken from the kitchen. He gets water from a pump by the sink. As the days pass, the Red Weed grows across the hole in the wall. On the fifteenth day a dog tries to get into the kitchen, but he frightens it away. The pit outside is silent, and when he finally looks out, he sees that the Martians have gone, leaving only the corpses of their human victims. At last he is able to escape, as the area is deserted, and neither Martians, nor their machines, nor other human beings are to be seen.

Book II, Chapter 6: The Work of Fifteen Days

Once he has escaped, the narrator realises the full magnitude of the disaster that has taken place; men are no longer in control of their own planet. He climbs through the thicknesses of the Red Weed in search of food. The growth of the Weed has caused the River Thames to flood; the Weed will soon, however, be destroyed by earthly bacteria. As he moves on towards central London, the narrator comes upon more scenes of desolation, but he discovers no signs of the Martians, or of other human survivors.

COMMENTARY: The information that the Red Weed is to be destroyed by the action of bacteria, against which terrestrial plants are to a certain extent immune, is Wells's first hint of the eventual fate of the Martians themselves.

NOTES AND GLOSSARY:
noisome: ill-smelling

navvies:	labourers employed in digging earthworks
gladiolus:	a species of garden flower
fronds:	large, leaf-like organs found in certain flowerless plants
cankering:	slowly decaying

Book II, Chapter 7: The Man on Putney Hill

The narrator spends the night at a deserted inn, brooding over the events of the past fortnight. Next day he goes on to Wimbledon Common, and comes across an armed man hiding in the bushes. It is the artilleryman who spent the night with him at Woking. The artilleryman explains that he has survived by hiding in the area conquered by the Martians, rather than joining the crowds of refugees. He anticipates that, after the initial destruction, the Martians will herd the remaining humans into prison camps. Those who remain free will be small groups of tough and determined men who recognise that civilisation has collapsed. He confides his own plan to form a guerrilla band, living underground in cellars, subways and drains. Eventually they will hope to take over a Martian Fighting Machine. The narrator soon observes that the artilleryman is not capable of carrying out his plans. They work together briefly at digging a tunnel, but the artilleryman soon tires of this work. They play cards together until evening, when the narrator goes out on to the roof and looks over London, which appears deserted. He decides to leave the artilleryman, and to go on by himself.

COMMENTARY: Much of this chapter takes the form of a dialogue, in which the artilleryman expounds his ideas on the survival of the human race under the Martian conquest. He argues that men have two choices: either to submit to enslavement by their new masters, or to form an underground resistance movement. If they choose to resist, they must be prepared to live as primitively as animals and to adopt ruthless tactics. Although the artilleryman is a dreamer and not a potential guerrilla leader, he has a highly intelligent grasp of the new situation brought about by the Martian invasion. But there is one basic flaw in his argument. He assumes that the Martians are already victorious, but this assumption will soon be shown to be false.

In the final paragraph of this chapter, the narrator's disillusionment with the artilleryman is expressed by the throwing away of the cigar.

NOTES AND GLOSSARY:
fetish prayers:	irrational and superstitious prayers
heathens:	holders of primitive or polytheistic religious beliefs
witless:	not possessing intelligence
cutlass:	a short, curved sword

culvert: a drain
dropping aitches: the Cockney or London habit of not sounding the letter 'h'
funk: panic
skedaddle: to run off
season-ticket train: train carrying office-workers to and from work
bar-loafers: idle drinkers
mashers: playboys or dandies
parleyed: negotiated
lackadaisical: sentimental, over-emotional
swipes: 'small beer'; a term of abuse
smithereens: small pieces
cloaca: drain
the old palace: Lambeth Palace in London, the official residence of the Archbishop of Canterbury (the head of the Church of England)
laburnums, pink mays, snowballs, arbor vitae, laurels, hydrangeas: garden flowers and shrubs
the Langham: a hotel in Regent Street, London
euchre, poker: card games
pasteboard: cardboard

Book II, Chapter 8: Dead London

The narrator walks through London, passing dead bodies, looted houses and a drunken man who curses at him. As he nears the city centre he hears a persistent howling noise, 'Ulla, ulla', in the distance. He breaks into a bar, finds food and drink, and sleeps until dark. Wandering northwards, he sees the hood of the Fighting Machine from which the howling comes. A dog with meat in his jaws comes toward him, and he finds a smashed Handling Machine, though it is too dark to see the remains of the dead Martian inside it. The howling of the first Martian suddenly stops. As night falls, the narrator runs away from the motionless Martians and seeks shelter. Next morning he creeps out and discovers that the invaders are all dead, killed by the earthly bacteria against which their bodies have no resistance. He sees the flying machine they had constructed before they were killed, and then, overcome with emotion, he wanders about the deserted city which has been miraculously saved from total destruction.

COMMENTARY: The poetic intensity of this chapter gives it a very high place in Wells's writings. The chapter both describes the deserted city and the discovery of the dying Martians, and gives the biological explanation for their defeat—a secret which, until this point, has been carefully hidden from the reader. The Martians, despite their terrible weapons, have none of the immunity which all the higher forms of life on Earth possess against micro-organic bacteria. (This may either be because such bacteria have never appeared on Mars, or because Martian science has eliminated them—see Book II, Chapter 2.) Wells's picture of the dying Martians has a poignant sadness, which is remarkable when we consider the terrible destruction they have caused. The chapter is full of the sense of degeneration and putrefaction, which may be observed even in such small details as the 'brutal type' of the drunkard's face, the maggots in the meat-safe of the public-house, and the rust which has grown over the railway lines after a fortnight's disuse. The emotional power of the scene comes from this sense of decay, and also from the narrator's feeling that he is the only observer of a deserted city. Despite his meetings with the artilleryman and the drunkard, he feels as if he were 'the last man left alive' in London. As the 'last man', he witnesses the death agony of the last Martian, and then feels the growth of new hope and pride in humanity as he knows that the invasion has been defeated.

NOTES AND GLOSSARY:
sweep: chimney-sweeper
provision and wineshops: food-shops and wineshops
magnum: a large bottle
Serpentine: the lake in London's Hyde Park
Samson: a biblical hero famed for his strength
putrefactive: causing decay
Sennacherib: the king of Assyria (705–681 B.C.). He had to retreat from Palestine when his army was destroyed by a plague. In the Bible, this is described as the work of an angel sent by God (II Chronicles 32). See also Byron's poem, 'The Destruction of Sennacherib'
enhaloed in: surrounded with

Book II, Chapter 9: Wreckage

The narrator is not the only man to learn of the Martians' overthrow. As the news of it spreads, there is world-wide rejoicing, and relief-workers and supplies come pouring into London. Meanwhile, the narrator wanders about the streets in a daze, until he is cared for by kindly people in St John's Wood. They tell him of the destruction of Leatherhead, where his family had gone, but he decides nonetheless to revisit his old house at Woking. He travels through the devastated countryside, observing the process of reoccupation and reconstruction that is already beginning. He arrives at his house, goes up to his study and comes across the paper he was writing when he first received news of the Martian invasion. The house is empty, but, hearing voices from the garden, he goes out to meet his wife, whom he had never expected to see again.

NOTES AND GLOSSARY:
advertisement stereo: advertisements printed from stereotypes or specially-designed plates
selenite: a crystalline mineral
French window: a door containing window-glass

Book II, Chapter 10: The Epilogue

The narrator's personal story is at an end and, in the style of a scientific report, he reflects on the Martian invasion and its consequences for mankind. The theory that Mars does not contain micro-organic bacteria is the most likely explanation for the death of the invaders. Neither the nature of the Black Smoke, nor the mechanism for generating the Heat-Ray, is yet understood. A specimen of the Martians themselves is preserved at the Natural History Museum. The danger of another attack from Mars remains, and it has been suggested that the Martians have landed on Venus. As a result of the invasion men's thoughts have been turned to the possibility of space travel, but it will be necessary to compete with the Martians if space travel is to become a reality. The narrator's experiences have left him with a strong feeling of doubt and insecurity, and as he goes about the streets of Woking and London he is still haunted by memories of the terrible experiences that he has recounted in *The War of the Worlds*.

COMMENTARY: The theme of this chapter is one of 'resurrection from the dead'. The narrator had thought that his wife was dead, that the city of London was dead, and that humanity was doomed to extermination by the Martians. None of these things has happened. The nightmare of the invasion is over—for the time being, at least—and the process of recovery is in hand.

Wells points out that a terrible experience such as the invasion from Mars might not be without its ultimate benefits for mankind.

NOTES AND GLOSSARY:
in conjunction: a planet is in conjunction when the sun stands between it and the Earth
sidereal space: the space in which the stars are situated
galvanized: stimulated by electricity

Part 3
Commentary

The starting-point: what would happen if...?

The War of the Worlds is a work of science fiction. Its starting-point is a piece of pure speculation—'What would happen if...?'—and its aim is to explore the logical consequences of that speculation as vividly and convincingly as possible.

The initial idea, as we learn from the Dedication, belonged not to Wells himself but to his brother Frank. On a peaceful country walk near Wells's home at Woking, Frank exclaimed: 'Suppose some beings from another planet were to drop out of the sky suddenly, and begin laying about them here!' To Wells, the suggestion was not a lurid daydream but an imaginative possibility to be explored with as much logic and as much descriptive vividness as he could command. His task, he later wrote, was to '*domesticate* the impossible hypothesis'; having admitted the one impossibility of an invasion from another planet, he would aim to 'keep everything else human and real'. *The War of the Worlds*, in modern terminology, belongs to the genre of science fiction as opposed to fantasy because the 'reality' of the story is continuously supported by appeals to the actual state of scientific knowledge, and to the actuality of English society, at the time when Wells was writing.

Thus the other planet had to be Mars; the invasion could be linked to a strange flash of light on Mars, which had recently been reported in the scientific press; and Wells set out to imagine exactly what the consequences might be for the people of England. The idea of an extra-terrestrial invasion of the Earth has various significant aspects:

1. It is the basis of an exciting story, full of suspense as we are naturally anxious for the fate of humanity under attack from an alien force.
2. The idea of alien, extra-terrestrial beings appeals powerfully to our sense of imaginative curiosity. What would they be like? What is their purpose in coming to Earth? How would they adapt to terrestrial conditions?
3. An invasion from outer space is an unprecedented challenge to the human beings who are subjected to it. How would present-day society meet that challenge? Which individuals and values would survive the test, and which would go under?

4. What would this meeting with another civilisation tell us about humanity as a whole? What would it reveal about Man's place in the world of nature? Supposing that Man survived the test, what effect would it have on the future course of human history?

In the following pages we shall deal separately with each of these aspects of the story. It is Wells's ability to weave all these aspects together into a vivid and readable narrative which constitutes the excellence of *The War of the Worlds* as a science-fiction story. Many more recent writers have taken the theme of extra-terrestrial invasion as a subject for their books. *The War of the Worlds* remains the classic treatment of this theme because of the breadth of vision that Wells possessed, and his ability to make the reader think as well as to tell him an exciting story.

The handling of the narrative

Fiction and history

The War of the Worlds is an *eye-witness account* of the Martian invasion. The excitement of the story owes much to the fact that the narrator sees the Martians at close quarters, and is often in personal danger. At the same time, Wells's narrator offers not just an eye-witness account, but an *objective history* of the events he describes. Wells's wish to give a broad view of the progress of the invasion meant that he had to narrate many more events than could have been seen by one man. On the whole, Wells solves this problem by having his narrator relate things that he heard later, or was told by others. Three whole chapters tell of the experiences of the narrator's younger brother, who makes his way from London to the East Coast while his brother remains trapped in North-West Surrey. In this part of the book the story is being told from two different viewpoints. The awkwardness of this arrangement may well be criticised, but it is clear why Wells adopted it. It was the easiest way in which he could combine 'eye-witness' immediacy with the description of such things as the way the news of the invasion reached London, the panic on the Great North Road and the battle between the Martians and the ship *Thunder Child*—all of which play an essential part in broadening the social and geographical scope of the story.

One other peculiarity of the narrative may be mentioned here, although few readers probably notice it. In Book I, Chapter 2 we read of the experiences of Ogilvy, the astronomer, as he approaches the Martian cylinder on Horsell Common just after dawn. Both Ogilvy and Henderson, the journalist to whom he relates his experiences, are killed later in the day. Neither has exchanged more than a few words with the narrator in the meantime. Wells's decision to include a detailed account of Ogilvy's experiences is one more sign of his willingness to disregard the strict rules of narrative form in the interests of vividness and immediacy.

The narrator

The narrator is a writer, living at Woking and 'busy upon a series of papers discussing the probable developments of moral ideas as civilisation progressed' (Book I, Chapter 1). He has some scientific training, is married and is learning to ride the bicycle. In all these characteristics he strongly resembles H. G. Wells himself in the year 1896. As the story goes on, however, one fact about the narrator becomes especially prominent. He is somebody who has survived the Martian invasion, where others have succumbed to it. His survival is partly due to good luck, and partly to certain qualities of character which may at times cast doubt on his qualifications as an impartial historian of the events he has undergone. As an eye-witness, therefore, the narrator is largely—but not wholly—reliable. (For further discussion of the character of the narrator, see the section on 'Characterisation' below.)

Style

Realism

By realism we mean the life-like quality of a work of fiction. The 'realistic' novelist portrays believable characters in familiar settings, and sets out to convince us that his story is a faithful picture of life as we know it, or of life as (under changed circumstances) we could expect it to be. Wells's belief that the science fiction writer must do everything possible to '*domesticate* the impossible hypothesis' led him to achieve a remarkable degree of realism in *The War of the Worlds*. Many factors contribute to the realistic effect of the narrative. The *geographical setting* is not only very accurate, but is so precisely detailed that the vast majority of readers, who are unfamiliar with the areas of England that Wells describes, are able to visualise these places sufficiently to become fully involved in the story. The *historical period* at which the novel is set is also vividly represented. Features of English life which are still very recognisable today—the suburban growth, the 'commuter' trains, the Sunday excursionists—are combined with other features such as the horse-drawn carriages, the hysterical curate and the pig-keeping landlord of the 'Spotted Dog' which take us back to the England of Charles Dickens. The social changes taking place around 1900 are registered, above all, in the new inventions coming into everyday use. The England of *The War of the Worlds* possesses the telegraph (but not the telephone), the bicycle (but not the motor-car) and a mass-market popular press (but no radio sets). The navy is being re-equipped with armour-plated battleships, while the army has got its first few machine-guns. The effect of so minutely detailed a treatment of historical time and place is not to dilute, but to heighten, the shock and horror of the Martian invasion.

Like other realistic writers, Wells combines the heightened and unusual events that he has to tell with the *commonplace details* of everyday life. Amid the violence of the invasion, the narrator does not neglect to tell us such details as where he slept and what he had to eat. The settled and comfortable quality of English middle-class life is represented by the descriptions of Woking and its surroundings, and by the narrator's casual conversations with his neighbours. The arrival of the invaders in such an ordinary environment increases the dramatic tension of the story. We see Wells's characters—nearly always typical figures, rather than carefully individualised people—reacting to sudden disaster in ways that we can anticipate and would expect. But as they do so, the familiar shape of society itself is disappearing and dissolving.

Wells's description of the collapse of society has, to some extent, the coolly analytic quality of *scientific observation*. His story has little that is flattering to human dignity, or to English pride. His realism extends to the Martians themselves, who are not seen as malignant or supernatural monsters, but as intelligent beings whose motives and behaviour are open to scientific explanation. There is little magic or mysticism in *The War of the Worlds*, either in the portrayal of the Martians or in the human response to their arrival, so that Wells's realism may be seen as an expression of a scientific and—in the philosophical sense—a materialist outlook on life.

'Documentation'

In the writing of history, 'documentation' is the process of providing evidence for what is said. Usually this evidence takes the form of written records dating from the time about which the historian is writing. The narrator of *The War of the Worlds* is a historian as well as an eye-witness of the Martian invasion. At some times he writes in the style of a journalist or newspaper reporter, while at other times he summarises newspaper reports which, he tells us, actually appeared at the time of the invasion. By 'documenting' what happened in this way, Wells seeks to increase the realism of his story. At the same time, the narrator invariably shows that the newspapers gave a mistaken or partial view of events. His function as a historian is to give a more correct view of the invasion than that put forward in earlier newspapers or pamphlets.

In some chapters Wells does not imitate the style of ordinary journalism, but that of a *scientific report*. This is especially the case in Book II, Chapter 2, where the narrator's position of observation in the ruined house enables him make a unique contribution to the scientific study of the Martians which takes place after the war. (The state of post-war 'Martian studies' is summed up in the Epilogue.) At such times Wells employs the specialised biological terminology which he himself learned as a biology student and teacher.

Imagination

The success with which Wells can persuade us that we are reading a history of real events is evidence of the power of his fictional imagination. It is interesting to consider his own account of how he wrote *The War of the Worlds*. He later recalled that he would 'take his bicycle of an afternoon and note the houses and cottages and typical inhabitants and passers-by, to be destroyed after tea by Heat-Ray or smothered in the Red Weed'. This suggests the care with which he studied the locations for the book, and also the vividness with which he imagined the events of his story. When he revisited certain places years later, Wells said, he chiefly remembered them as the scenes of battles in the Martian war. The realism of *The War of the Worlds* is sometimes so intense that it can have the effect of a hallucination, for the reader as well as for Wells himself. *The War of the Worlds* is in fact more memorable than many eye-witness descriptions of actual battles. Such vividness results from the emotional engagement of Wells's writing, and above all from his success in evoking the emotions of wonder and fear that the narrator feels.

Plot

In the comments which follow, the plot of *The War of the Worlds* will be regarded as the means by which Wells controls the reader's emotional response to the story of the Martian invasion. The order in which the events are told helps to preserve a balance between intense emotions of excitement and horror, on the one hand, and a reassuring sense of normality on the other. The Martians are frightening creatures, and their battle with humanity is not a conventional war but a struggle between two biological species, which at times reminds us of the Victorian poet Tennyson's famous description of 'nature red in tooth and claw'. It is through the plot that Wells exercises artistic control over his story, arranging the events in such a way as to keep their violence from becoming excessive. His aim is to hold the reader's interest at all times, and to keep him guessing about what will happen next.

Book I

In 'Book I: The Coming of the Martians', Wells takes us from the launching of the invasion to the moment at which the Martian conquest appears to be complete. In the opening chapter, things are seen calmly and at a distance; the narrator looks through the telescope at Mars, far away in space, and around him is the silence of the observatory. The short chapters which follow show how the peace of Woking and its surroundings was shattered by the arrival of the Martians and their use of the Heat-Ray. During the rest of Book I we see the Martians advance, spreading ruthless destruction wherever they go. Three dramatic episodes describe the scenes of panic that the invaders cause. These are: Chapters 9 and 10, in which the Heat-Ray turns on Maybury Hill and the Fighting Machines make their first appearance; Chapter 12, in which Weybridge and Shepperton are destroyed; and Chapters 16 and 17, describing the exodus from London and the battle between the Martians and the ship *Thunder Child*. But these chapters are interspersed with calmer episodes (Chapters 11, 13 and 15) in which the narrator sums up what has happened and waits for the Martians' next move. By the end of Book I, the swift and shocking destruction of humanity has been both experienced at first hand, and reported in more general terms by a narrator who can foresee no escape from the Martian terror.

Book II

In 'Book II: The Earth Under the Martians' things do not develop in the way that might have been expected. Wells could have shown the forces of mankind rallying, recovering their strength and finding some way to defeat the Martian enemy. The artilleryman in Chapter 7 outlines a guerrilla strategy for fighting the Martians, but the task seems hopeless. Instead, the Martians are defeated by the action of bacteria, and not by men. But in the meantime they have become more comprehensible creatures to us, so that by the time they are defeated they are capable of arousing our sympathy.

The narrator's imprisonment in the ruined house puts a stop to his narrative of the Martians' advance, and forces him instead to study the invaders closely. Despite his horrifying discovery that they feed by sucking human blood, his description of the Martians is full of wonder at the strangeness of the biological features he observes. He suggests that the Martians are superior to men in some ways, though they may seem inferior in others. This impression is reinforced by the emphasis on human weakness in the characters of the curate and the artilleryman.

When the narrator escapes, his first thoughts are of his own safety, but soon curiosity overcomes him. In the now-desolate city, what has become of the Martians? The eeriness of Chapter 8 ('Dead London') comes to a climax with the discovery of the Martians dead and dying, and wailing 'Ulla, ulla' in their agony. It is for the Martians, and no longer for mankind, that we feel sympathy in this moment of defeat.

The ending of *The War of the Worlds* will be discussed in further detail below (page 53). The book ends with the rebuilding of society and the slow re-emergence of human confidence. After the emotional shock of seeing life reduced to its biological basis—above all, in the images of decay and putrefaction which accompany the Martians' downfall—the novel ends on a note of reassurance, which is summed up in the narrator's reunion with his wife.

The portrayal of the Martians

Repulsiveness

The most obvious characteristic of the Martians is their alien nature; they are completely outside Man's experience. This is expressed, first and foremost, through their physical repulsiveness. In general they resemble reptiles and molluscs, especially the octopus, rather than any mammalian species; but Wells adds certain details which suggest repulsive aspects of insects, animals and even of plants. In this they anticipate the so-called 'bug-eyed monsters' imagined by the twentieth-century authors of science-fiction films and comic strips. Wells also offers biological explanations for the physiology of the Martians, and these explanations qualify to some extent the impression of almost obscene ugliness that is initially created.

One further cause of the Martians' repulsiveness is their inability to move about normally on Earth, due to the difference between the Earth's gravity and that of Mars. It is partly to overcome this that they employ their colossal Fighting Machines.

Intelligence

The other major characteristic of the Martians is their intelligence. In the first paragraph they are introduced as 'intelligences greater than Man's and yet as mortal as his own', 'minds that are to our minds as ours are to those of the beasts that perish, intellects vast and cool and unsympathetic', regarding the Earth with 'envious eyes'. The idea that Man is being watched over by beings of greater intelligence (a comparison with the Christian God is implied by Wells) is itself a source of wonder and fear. And Wells insists that an intelligence which is alien to our own will also have no respect for human feelings and values. A direct result of the Martians' intelligence, in his view, is their cruelty.

Is the Martians' cruelty necessary?

It is perfectly possible that visitors from other planets would be well-disposed towards Man. Thus there is some justice in the charge that writers who portray extra-terrestrial creatures as monstrous and cruel do so for sensational effect. There is, undoubtedly, a parallel between science fiction horror stories, and war propaganda which encourages us to see other nations, races or social classes as 'monstrous' and 'repulsive'. (From the point of view of such propaganda, 'we' are invariably righteous, peace-loving and innocent.) However, Wells does not contrast the cruelty of the Martians with the innocence of Man, since he emphasises that men are quite as cruel as the Martians are. Thus the cruelty of the Martians reflects Wells's beliefs about Man and Nature.

The cruelty of nature

As a late nineteenth-century biology student, Wells had learned that violence and cruelty were inherent in nature. He was familiar with the habits of predatory species of birds and mammals, and with the description of man himself as a carnivorous mammal. However horrible to us, the blood-sucking habits of the Martians have many parallels in nature. The theory of evolution had shown all life as a relentless struggle for the means of subsistence, and had revealed the health of each species as the result of continuous competition with other species. The cruelty of the Martians expresses Wells's appalled and fascinated contemplation of these biological factors.

The cruelty of Man

Wells takes great care to emphasise that the Martians' violence and cruelty are no worse than those of Man himself. Men have often been appallingly cruel toward two categories of creatures: other animals, and people whom they consider 'inferior'. Wells uses metaphors and similes throughout the text to remind us of these forms of human cruelty. Thus the human beings subject to the Martian invasion are compared to bisons, dodos, rabbits and even frogs. They are also compared to the native inhabitants of Tasmania, who were wiped out by European settlers during the nineteenth century. In this colonial war the Whites 'treated the Aborigines as sub-human, seizing their hunting-grounds, depleting their food supply, attacking the women, and killing the Aborigines without provocation. Tasmanian attempts to resist were met with the superior weaponry and force of the Europeans' (*Encyclopaedia Britannica*). The parallel with *The War of the Worlds* is distressingly exact.

Does this mean that *The War of the Worlds* should be read as an anti-imperialist book, in which the Europeans, and specifically the English, are made to suffer the cruelties that they themselves have inflicted on others? In fact, *The War of the Worlds* is too ambiguous to be read as a political tract. While the terror caused by the Martians is vividly portrayed, Wells does not condemn what they are doing. Instead, he suggests that it is a natural response to the threat posed to their survival by the cooling of Mars, their native planet. Faced with the choice between conquering Earth and a slow extinction on Mars, the Martians set out to conquer Earth with whatever ruthlessness may be necessary. The question of their cruelty is therefore seen from two points of view (the terrestrial and the Martian) and involves a dramatically effective conflict between two scales of values (those dictated by *humanitarianism*, and those dictated by *biological necessity*). It is not part of Wells's purpose to choose between these scales of values. (In fact, the opposition may be a false one, since it is only the species, and never individuals, who are in a position to follow the dictates of 'biological necessity' in the sense in which it has been used above. This is why *The War of the Worlds* does not offer any really profound examination of the moral and political issues raised by the Martians' cruelty.)

The Martians and evolution

In Book II, Chapter 2, the narrator mentions an article written in November or December 1893, by a 'certain speculative writer of quasi-scientific repute', which 'did forecast for Man a final structure not unlike the actual Martian condition'. The article, written by H. G. Wells himself, was called 'The Man of the Year Million'. In it Wells had speculated on the evolutionary changes which might have transformed human beings in a million years' time. The development of machinery, he argued, would make arms and legs unnecessary, while the need for a stomach and digestive system would be superseded by 'immersion in a tub of nutritive fluid'. The human body would shrivel up apart from its two essential organs—an enormous brain and enormous hands. This grotesquely humorous vision is the origin of the Martians in *The War of the Worlds*.

The Martians' lack of a digestive system lifts them above the fluctuations of mood and emotion which affect humanity. They are colder, more calculating and more purely selfish beings. Having done away with any extensive system of muscles, they do not need to sleep. Sexual distinctions are unknown among them, thus removing one more source of emotional instability. They communicate with one another by direct telepathic means, and not through the medium of speech. All these developments are summed up by Wells as the 'suppression of the animal side of the organism by the intelligence'.

What is disguised by the repulsive alienness and cruelty of the Martians, then, is that they resemble the *men of the far future*. Men are 'just in the beginning of the evolution that the Martians have worked out'. In viewing the cruelty, the technological skill and the terrible power of the Martians, we are viewing what Man may one day evolve into. This point is central to Wells's attitude of moral ambiguity towards the Martians, which has already been noted.

Technology

Martian technology has reached a stage where the availability of machines has itself determined the evolutionary process. On Earth, the Martians appear to be almost helpless without their machines. The descriptions of their machines have as much, if not more, visual impact than the descriptions of the Martians themselves. Most memorable of all are the vast three-legged Fighting Machines, each standing higher than a house and directed by a Martian perched at the top inside an armoured hood. The Fighting Machines first appear on the night of the storm (Book I, Chapter 10), and again during the destruction of Weybridge and Shepperton. The Martians have other machines, such as the Handling Machines, as well as highly destructive weapons which foreshadow modern inventions such as the laser beam and poison gas. The invaders' industrial capability is shown by the aluminium-extracting plant that they set up in the pit beside the ruined house, and their weird mechanical ingenuity appears in the fact that they have done without the invention of the wheel.

In many ways the Martians in their Fighting Machines remind us, quite simply, of the *giants* that are found in traditional myths, folk-tales and fairy-stories. Their gigantism is a symbol (repeated in one of Wells's later science fiction novels, *The Food of the Gods*) of a level of evolutionary development and technological progress which has dwarfed the achievements of present-day Man. Because the Martians and their machines represent the promise of the future, they are meant to arouse in the reader a sense of horrified fascination.

The response to the invasion

Wells's attack on Victorian complacency

Wells is as much concerned with the way in which human beings respond to the invasion as with the nature of the Martians themselves. Writing towards the end of one of the most peaceful periods of English history, he imagines what would happen if England were subjected to war and destruction. Later, looking back after the shattering experience of the First World War of 1914-18, Wells wrote that the intention of *The War of the Worlds* had been to 'comment on the false securities and fatuous self-satisfaction of the everyday life—as we knew it then'. The speed of the social collapse which follows the Martian invasion is one of the book's most remarkable features. Within a few days, millions of people have left their homes, the government has ceased to function, and the general panic is reflected in the curate's belief that the end of the world has come. The moral of the Martian invasion is that any society, even one as prosperous and self-confident as Victorian Britain, could be threatened by sudden and unforeseen disaster. Such a disaster need not involve an invasion from outer space; it could take the form of a war, a natural event such as an earthquake, or a political revolution. The experience of disaster is a 'moment of truth' in which the social structure—not just of Victorian Britain, but of modern civilisation as a whole—is shown to be precarious and insecure. Like a house built on shaky foundations, it could crash without warning on the heads of its inhabitants.

The armed forces

One of the lessons of the invasion is the helplessness of the British armed forces in the face of the Martians' weaponry. At the time when Wells was writing, the army and navy had not been engaged in a major war (with the exception of the Crimean War) since the defeat of Napoleon in 1815. Many observers believed that the British forces were ill-equipped, especially in the face of the new industrial and military power of Germany. The German Navy was growing fast, while the superiority of their land forces had been shown in the Franco-Prussian War of 1870. A large number of 'future war' novels, beginning with Sir George Chesney's *The Battle of Dorking* (1871), set out to warn the English public of the danger. Considered as a warning of this kind, *The War of the Worlds* is an impressive forecast of the experience of 'total war' as it has been known in the twentieth century. Using new and terrible destructive weapons, the Martians mount an outright assault upon the civilian population. Their weapons include mobile Fighting Machines and the Black Smoke (suggesting, respectively, the tanks and poison gas which came into use in the 1914-18 war). The army and navy are quite unprepared for what happens. (The army is, in fact, initially called out to *protect* the Martians from the crowd on Horsell Common.) They put up a courageous fight but are soon overwhelmed, so that the only hope of resisting the Martians in the long term would have been by guerrilla methods, such as those proposed by the artilleryman.

The civilian population

Since the Martians unleash a 'total war', the rout of the civilian population provides many of the most graphic scenes in *The War of the Worlds*. At first the people of England cannot believe the danger they are in. The social organisation of the towns and cities seems too massive and stable to be overwhelmed by a sudden disaster. Wells brilliantly traces how the 'tidal wave' of fear spreads across the country, how the system of peacetime communications collapses and the roads and railways are choked with refugees. Book II, Chapter 8 ('Dead London') suggests that a city or metropolis is a living organism subject, like any other organism, to sudden death. Wells uses several kinds of imagery to intensify his portrayal of disaster and collapse. Notable is the imagery of fire and smoke (corresponding to the Martians' Heat-Ray and Black Smoke) which gives the devastated landscape the appearance of the Christian inferno or hell.

Characterisation

In *The War of the Worlds*, as in other science fiction novels, the characterisation is not highly developed. Subtly individualised characters would be out of place in a novel dealing with the relationship between humanity and an extra-terrestrial species, since in this context it is the most general features of human behaviour which become important. As the novelist and critic C. S. Lewis once wrote, 'Every good writer knows that the more unusual the scenes and events of his story are, the slighter, the more ordinary, the more typical his persons should be'. To a large extent Wells followed this principle in *The War of the Worlds*, with the result that virtually every aspect of characterisation in the book relates to a single theme—that of the *problem of survival*. In a situation of sudden disaster, certain kinds of behaviour will help to ensure survival, and other kinds of behaviour will hinder it. What are they?

The narrator

The narrator regards himself as pre-eminently a survivor. He even comes to see himself as 'The Last Man Left Alive' (Book II, Chapter 9), regardless of the huge area of the world left untouched by the Martian attack. (At this point he is, in fact, demented, and owes his survival to the charity of others.) From the beginning of the story he emphasises his own awareness of danger, in contrast to the suicidal behaviour and slow-witted disbelief of others. His determination to protect himself and his wife is seen in the swiftness with which he secures the cart belonging to the landlord of the Spotted Dog (Book I, Chapter 9). He does nothing to warn the landlord of their common danger, and we are left in no doubt as to the ruthlessness of his action, since the landlord is found dead that same night.

Later on, when trapped in the ruined house with the curate, he acts still more ruthlessly, stunning his companion with the blade of an axe to prevent him from giving away their whereabouts to the Martians. While this may be justified as a legitimate act of self-defence, it is also an expression of his whole attitude to the curate, which has been intolerant and contemptuous from the beginning. However 'reasonable' this may be, it leaves a somewhat unpleasant impression.

Although he is portrayed as a philosopher concerned with the 'probable development of moral ideas as civilisation progressed', the narrator seems neither a very moral nor a very far-sighted person. He does not foresee, for example, that Leatherhead is far too close to Woking for it to be a safe place to leave his wife. (His younger brother, who escapes across the North Sea, is more perspicacious.) He seems to alternate between a determination to escape from the Martians, and an intense curiosity about them. He does not pause to consider the long-term prospects for humanity under the Martian conquest, as the artilleryman does. But his combination of curiosity and determination to survive are sufficient to keep him in close proximity to the Martians, without becoming their victim.

Ironically enough, the narrator's basic selfishness is not unlike the 'selfish intelligence' of the Martians themselves. As with the Martians, it is not easy to approve of some of his actions; on the other hand, his success in staying alive makes it difficult to condemn them either. But it is notable that, among the other main characters, the curate and the artilleryman both represent specific types of human weakness, which the reader can join with the narrator in condemning. By contrast, Wells fails in *The War of the Worlds* to suggest the acts of self-sacrifice and of unselfish moral heroism of which ordinary human beings are capable in moments of crisis. Those who die are regarded (with a few exceptions, such as the crew of the *Thunder Child*) as pathetic victims rather than as heroes.

The curate

The curate is an unpleasant, and also a rather unconvincing character. In psychological terms his behaviour is quite credible, since he is shown as being mentally ill from the moment when the narrator first meets him. But in making him representative of the religious mentality, and in giving him such a large part in the story, Wells seems to give way to anti-religious prejudice. As a thinker he often loosely divided humanity into two groups, the forward-looking (scientists, technicians etc.)

and the backward-looking (priests, politicians, lawyers etc.). This was a useful propaganda device in his battle against English conservatism, but in his fiction it could easily become a vehicle for simple prejudice. Into his portrayal of the whining, selfish and fear-maddened curate, Wells poured all the vehemence of his rejection of the religion in which he had been brought up.

Other characters: the artilleryman

Many of Wells's other characters are purely functional. These include the narrator's wife and younger brother, Ogilvy the astronomer, Henderson the journalist, and the two middle-class ladies, Mrs and Miss Elphinstone, who are saved from attack by robbers. The one other character of importance in the book is the artilleryman. He first appears in Book I, Chapter 11, and reappears as a dreamer full of ambitious schemes to save humanity in Book II, Chapter 7. What he offers is a more extreme version of the narrator's own 'survival ethics'. He divides humanity into those who are over-civilised and those who are prepared to revert to the ruthlessness of the savage. Brutally dismissing the former as fair prey for the Martians, he dreams of leading a guerrilla band of tough individuals to ensure the survival of the race and its values and, if possible, to capture a Martian Fighting Machine. Had the invasion continued, his plan might have been put to the test. But as it is, he is revealed as a lazy and boastful individual whose own efforts at resistance are laughable. And like everyone else, he has failed to notice the signs that the Martians are not to be victorious after all.

General themes and ideas: the 'dethronement of Man'

Man's relation to nature

The narrator speaks in Book II, Chapter 6 of his 'sense of dethronement', his 'persuasion that I was no longer a master, but an animal among the animals, under the Martian heel'. *The War of the Worlds* portrays a biological reversal, which threatens Man's comfortable position of dominance over the rest of the animal kingdom. Once the Martians arrive on Earth it seems that human beings are the losers, not the winners in the struggle for existence. Wells uses animal similes and metaphors throughout the story to emphasise this ironic new state of affairs. For example, one of the Sunday newspapers complacently compares the Martian landing to a 'menagerie suddenly let loose in a village' (Book I, Chapter 14). But the Martians, in their turn, destroy

Leatherhead as thoughtlessly as 'a boy might crush an anthill' (Book II, Chapter 9). From the invaders' point of view, men are as tiny and insignificant as the 'infusoria under the microscope' (Book I, Chapter 1) are to us.

Nature consists both of impersonal forces and of living beings. The Martians are spurred to leave their own planet by the threat of a new Ice Age, and their coming to Earth is reminiscent of a natural disaster such as an earthquake or a tidal wave. But the narrator is also shown experiencing the calm of nature—the stillness of the night, or the silence of London when its inhabitants have fled. In addition, he observes the resilience of animal species, such as the birds and the dog and cat which return to the pit next to the ruined house when the Martians have left it (Book II, Chapter 5). Most resilient of all are the disease bacteria, which attack and kill the Martians themselves. These bacteria, which are so tiny as to escape most men's notice, are the key to human survival. The fact that they succeed in defeating the Martians, where human efforts fail, is Wells's ultimate criticism of the complacency of men.

The future of Man

The War of the Worlds, like Wells's other works of science fiction, is a prophetic book which aims to undermine the complacency of men about their future prospects. It shows that the self-confidence of late Victorian England is misplaced, and that Man's present mastery of nature may be short-lived. It questions the permanence of modern capitalist industrial civilisation, and suggests how easily a highly-organised nation-state like Britain in the nineteenth century could disintegrate under pressure from an unforeseen enemy. *The War of the Worlds*, therefore, expresses the anxieties of men as they looked forward at the end of the nineteenth century, and may be seen as a fantastic vision or prophecy of the possible course of twentieth-century history. It may equally be seen as expressing some of the anxieties of men in the industrialised nations today.

Wells adds, however, that the Martian invasion may have brought great benefits to humanity. It led to a complete change in human attitudes, bringing great advances in science, the possibility of space travel, international co-operation and a new sense of purpose. In the very long term, however, the cooling of Mars must be repeated on Earth, and men will be faced with the choice of trying to settle elsewhere, as the Martians did, or of engaging in a hopeless struggle to survive on a planet no longer hospitable to them.

The ending of *The War of the Worlds*

The death of the Martians

As we have seen, the death of the Martians is hardly a triumph for mankind. On the one hand, their defeat was the work of bacteria and not of human beings, while, on the other, the defeated Martians may be seen as resembling the men of the far future. The nature of their death is reminiscent of the mysterious plagues (such as the Black Death in fourteenth-century Europe) which have, from time to time, swept across whole continents. In the Martians' death agony we see their essential loneliness (why were so few cylinders launched from Mars?), and also the cruelty of the natural processes to which men and Martians are both subject. It is because of the similarities that have been suggested between the Martians and humanity that the death of the supposedly invincible invaders, amid the silence of the deserted city, is so moving.

The narrator's reunion with his wife

Despite warnings that the defeat of the Martians may be only a temporary relief, *The War of the Worlds* closes with a conventional Victorian 'happy ending'. We are never told how the narrator's wife could have escaped from the complete destruction of Leatherhead. She did escape, however, and the narrator, and presumably most of Wells's readers, are satisfied. The reunion fits in with the mood of reconstruction, indeed of resurrection from the dead, in Book II, Chapter 9. The final paragraphs of Wells's novel remind us that her survival must be set against the continuing memory of the nightmare that the narrator has experienced:

> I sit in my study writing by lamplight, and suddenly I see again the healing valley below set with writhing flames, and feel the house behind and about me empty and desolate. I go out into the Byfleet Road, and vehicles pass me, a butcher-boy in a cart, a cabful of visitors, a workman on a bicycle, children going to school, and suddenly they become vague and unreal, and I hurry again with the artilleryman through the hot, brooding silence. Of a night I see the black powder darkening the silent streets, and the contorted bodies shrouded in that layer; they rise upon me tattered and dog-bitten. They gibber and grow fiercer, paler, uglier, mad distortions of humanity at last, and I wake, cold and wretched, in the darkness of the night.

In these sentences there is summed up the vividness of *The War of the Worlds*. A literal nightmare which the narrator has experienced becomes an image of horror, shared by every reader.

Popularity and influence

'The thing from outer space'

The War of the Worlds remains Wells's most popular science fiction novel, although by common agreement it comes second to *The Time Machine* in terms of literary quality. Evidence of its popularity is to be found in the large quantity of adaptations and imitations of Wells's story that continues to appear. For example, most of the American science fiction films of the 1950s and 1960s dealing with lurid 'things from outer space' could be traced back to *The War of the Worlds*.

Stories in which human beings are threatened by repulsive and alien creatures provide a safe outlet for the violent and aggressive tendencies of modern Man. There is no doubt that part of the appeal of *The War of the Worlds* is based on our enjoyment of imaginary tales of suffering and disaster. But Wells (unlike most of his imitators) assumes an intelligent reader who will be troubled by the questions of morality that his story raises, and who will not see the defeat of the Martians as a matter of simple revenge. In the majority of imitations of Wells's story, the strands of deeper meaning are absent, and the result is a mindless war-story which serves to reinforce popular prejudices and conventional attitudes, rather than questioning them as Wells attempted to do.

What is most noticeably missing from these stories of 'bug-eyed monsters' is the specifically *scientific* content of *The War of the Worlds*. Instead of chapters of biological and astronomical reasoning, we are confronted with horrifying creatures who are motivelessly hostile towards mankind. They are apt to be defeated, not by the bacteria which were a crucial discovery of nineteenth-century medicine, but by a miraculously gifted young hero who relies on magical luck and super-human skill to defeat the enemy. The difference between Wells's book and such commercially-motivated imitations will be obvious.

The War of the Worlds and contemporary fiction

The works of some contemporary writers of science fiction who have dealt with the theme of a Martian invasion of Earth should not be confused with the popular imitations discussed above. These are writers who have added new dimensions to Wells's story. Two recent examples of this are Kurt Vonnegut's *The Sirens of Titan* (1959) and Arkady and Boris Strugatsky's story 'The Second Martian Invasion' (1966). Christopher Priest's *The Space Machine* (1976) is an affectionate re-writing of Wells's story which expresses a modern writer's nostalgia for Victorian England. These adaptations of Wells's idea testify to the continuing literary and popular appeal of *The War of the Worlds*

Part 4
Hints for study

Points to select for detailed study

General approach

Each of the following aspects of *The War of the Worlds* may be studied separately (though they are all, of course, related to one another). The critical commentaries provided in Parts 2 and 3 of these Notes will help you to study these aspects of the text in detail. You should note that the headings used to group together the different aspects follow the order observed in Part 3. Each section below may therefore be studied together with the corresponding section in Part 3, and you should refer to Part 3 for an explanation of the terms used. You will find it helpful to compile a list of passages in the text which illustrate the aspect selected.

Genre

The 'genre' of *The War of the Worlds*—the type of story that it is—is science fiction. What does it have in common with other science fiction you have read? In what ways does the story illustrate Wells's knowledge of science? In what ways is this scientific knowledge essential to the story?

Narrative viewpoint and style

What is the setting of *The War of the Worlds*? What narrative viewpoints does Wells adopt? What sort of person is the narrator? Does he give a wholly reliable view of events? What do you take to be the strengths and weaknesses of Wells's style? How important is the use of similes and metaphors in the narrative?

Plot

What are the main turning-points in the story? Which chapters strike you as the most dramatic? Does Wells succeed in his aim of making the story plausible? What are the principal emotions that Wells evokes in the course of the story?

The Martians

What are the Martians like? What explanations are given for their appearance and behaviour? What are the most important features of their technology? Why did they invade Earth, and how are they defeated? How effective do you find Wells's descriptions of the Martians to be?

Human behaviour and characterisation

1. *Social behaviour:* What is the initial reaction to the Martian landings? How do men try to resist the Martians? How successful are they? How does Wells portray the processes of social collapse, and, later, of reconstruction?
2. *Individual behaviour:* How effective is Wells's characterisation in *The War of the Worlds*? What is its purpose? Analyse the portrayal of the narrator, the curate and the artilleryman. What parts are played by the minor characters in the story?

General themes and ideas

The general themes and ideas of *The War of the Worlds* arise from a consideration of the relations between the Martians and humanity. How would you summarise these general themes and ideas? What does the book suggest about modern Man's relation to nature, to other terrestrial species, to extra-terrestrial beings, and to the universe? What means does Wells use to communicate these themes to the reader? What long-term effects does the Martian invasion have on Man? How do you think Wells's attitudes as revealed in *The War of the Worlds* strike us today?

The ending

How effective is the ending of *The War of the Worlds*? How do the events which terminate the book relate to the rest of the story? How does the reader react to these events?

Critical assessment

What are the strengths and weaknesses of Wells's book as a whole? What do you like and/or dislike about it? Compare and contrast *The War of the Worlds* with (i) any other book by Wells that you have read, or (ii) any other novel or film on a similar theme with which you are familiar.

Selection of key quotations

The following is a selection of passages which contribute significantly to the overall meaning of *The War of the Worlds*. You should familiarise yourself with each quotation and its context. Where does it come in *The War of the Worlds*? What part does it play in the narrative? Which of the aspects of the book listed above does it relate to, and in what ways?

For quotation in essays or examination answers you should make your own list of passages and phrases which illustrate particular points or themes of the book.

(*a*) It is curious to recall some of the mental habits of those departed days. At most, terrestrial men fancied there might be other men upon Mars, perhaps inferior to themselves and ready to welcome a missionary enterprise. Yet, across the gulf of space, minds that are to our minds as ours are to those of the beasts that perish, intellects vast and cool and unsympathetic, regarded this earth with envious eyes, and slowly and surely drew their plans against us. And early in the twentieth century came the great disillusionment. (Book I, Chapter 1)

(*b*) And before we judge of them too harshly, we must remember what ruthless and utter destruction our own species has wrought, not only upon animals, such as the vanished bison and the dodo, but upon its own inferior races. The Tasmanians, in spite of their human likeness, were entirely swept out of existence in a war of extermination waged by European immigrants, in the space of fifty years. Are we such apostles of mercy as to complain if the Martians warred in the same spirit? (Book I, Chapter 1)

(*c*) 'They have done a foolish thing,' said I, fingering my wineglass. 'They are dangerous, because no doubt they are mad with terror. Perhaps they expected to find no living things—certainly no intelligent living things. A shell in the pit,' said I, 'if the worst comes to the worst, will kill them all.' (Book I, Chapter 7)

(*d*) Never before in the history of the world had such a mass of human beings moved and suffered together. The legendary hosts of Goths and Huns, the hugest armies Asia has ever seen, would have been but a drop in that current. And this was no disciplined march; it was a stampede—a stampede gigantic and terrible—without order and without a goal, six million people, unarmed and unprovisioned, driving headlong. It was the beginning of the rout of civilisation, of the massacre of mankind. (Book I, Chapter 17)

(*e*) There is many a true word written in jest, and here in the Martians we have beyond dispute the actual accomplishment of such a suppression of the animal side of the organism by the intelligence. To me it is quite credible that the Martians may be descended from beings not unlike ourselves, by a gradual development of brain and hands (the latter giving rise to the two bunches of delicate tentacles at last) at the expense of the rest of the body. Without the body the brain would of course become a more selfish intelligence, without any of the emotional substratum of the human being. (Book II, Chapter 2)

(*f*) I felt the first inkling of a thing that presently grew quite clear in my mind, that oppressed me for many days, a sense of dethronement, a persuasion that I was no longer a master, but an animal among the animals, under the Martian heel. (Book II, Chapter 6)

(*g*) At any rate, whether we expect another invasion or not, our views of the human future must be greatly modified by these events. (Book II, Chapter 10)

Specimen answers

Four specimen answers are included here in order to suggest what is the best way of organising your material when faced with two of the commonest types of examination question. Specimen answer (A) is included in full. Specimen answers (B), (C) and (D) indicate the points which might be covered in a continuous essay written in response to the questions.

Question (A)

Write a brief commentary on the following passage, indicating both its immediate context in the book, and its relation to an appreciation of *The War of the Worlds* as a whole:

> One only has to imagine the fate of those batteries towards Esher, waiting so tensely in the twilight, as well as one may. Survivors there were none. One may picture the orderly expectation, the officers alert and watchful, the gunners ready, the ammunition piled to hand, the limber gunners with their horses and wagons, the groups of civilian spectators standing as near as they were permitted, the evening stillness; the ambulances and hospital tents, with the burnt and wounded from Weybridge; then the dull resonance of the shots the Martians fired, and the clumsy projectile whirling over the trees and houses, and smashing amidst the neighbouring fields.

ANSWER:

In this passage the narrator describes the futile resistance put up by the army as the Martians advanced from their landing-sites near Woking towards London. Immediately after this, Wells describes the panic which develops among the people of London as they realise that the army is powerless to protect them. The army is helpless because the

Martians never come within range of their guns. Instead, they fire their 'clumsy projectiles' containing the Black Smoke, which suffocates all who breathe it. Wells here anticipates twentieth-century poison-gas warfare, and suggests how modern technology can be used to change the nature of war and to overwhelm armies equipped with more old-fashioned weapons. At this point in the story the Martians, armed with the Heat-Ray as well as the Black Smoke, appear to be completely invincible.

In this paragraph the narrator is not describing something which he himself saw. He invites us to imagine the fate of the 'batteries towards Esher', and paints a vivid picture of the scene. Here we see Wells attempting to combine an objective history of the events of the invasion, written with hindsight after the Martian defeat, with an 'eye-witness account' which makes these events seem more concrete and real. The defeat of the gunners is a pathetic and even poignant spectacle; they are overcome by the Black Smoke without firing a shot. The twilight setting, which Wells emphasises in this passage, might be symbolically understood as the twilight of humanity itself. Soon the civilisation of Victorian England will be reduced to chaos, and the narrator will write of his 'sense of dethronement', as he and the other survivors of defeated humanity have to accustom themselves to living 'under the Martian heel'.

Question (B)

Give an account of the battle between the Martians and the British, describing the Martians' tactics and the human attempts to counter them.

ANSWER:
1. The Martians begin the battle by turning the Heat-Ray on the harmless crowds of people on Horsell Common.
2. Once they have erected their Fighting Machines, they begin to lay waste to the surrounding countryside.
3. Wells describes the battle between the Martian Fighting Machines and human artillery at Shepperton. The gunners manage to destroy one of the Martians.
4. As a result of this, the Martians withdraw to Horsell Common.
5. Meanwhile, the army makes preparations to defend the approaches to London.
6. The Martians march on London, using a new weapon—the Black Smoke—to take the army by surprise.
7. The last effective resistance is that of the naval torpedo-ram *Thunder Child*.

60 · Hints for study

8. Soon the Martians are in control of south-east England. The army and navy have been defeated, and only individual human beings like the artilleryman are left to continue the fight.
9. But Wells finally shows that bacteria can succeed where men have failed.

Question (C)

Discuss how Wells uses characterisation in *The War of the Worlds* to show the different ways in which men respond to the Martian invasion.

ANSWER:
1. *The War of the Worlds* is full of minor characters (give examples). Each of these characters stands in some relation to the overall theme of the human response to the invasion.
2. Nevertheless, three main characters stand out—the curate, the artilleryman and the narrator himself.
3. The curate is shown as a religious fanatic who, under the stress of the invasion, appears to go completely insane.
4. The artilleryman dreams of becoming a guerrilla leader, but is shown as boastful and lazy.
5. The narrator acts more sensibly than the artilleryman or the curate, although his behaviour sometimes seems selfish and unheroic.
6. Nevertheless, it is through his eyes that we tend to judge the other characters.
7. Despite his human weaknesses, the narrator is a philosopher and writer who is able to observe and understand the Martians themselves. One of his main functions in the story is to express Wells's own reflections on the significance of the Martian invasion.
8. In conclusion, the characters of *The War of the Worlds* are types rather than individuals. Wells is more interested in showing the varieties of response to a common danger, than in exploring the nature of individual psychology.

Question (D)

'*Extra-terrestrial* is the key word of the whole story. And in the later horrors, excellently as they are done, we lose the feeling of it.' (C. S. Lewis on *The War of the Worlds*). Do you agree with C. S. Lewis's criticism of the book?

ANSWER:
1. The idea of extra-terrestrial beings such as the Martians is introduced in the very first paragraph of *The War of the Worlds*.

2. The existence of the Martians is contrasted with the 'infinite complacency' of men.
3. Wells describes the strangeness and repulsiveness of the Martians and their machines when we first see them.
4. He adds to these descriptions later in the book.
5. Nevertheless, it is true that many of the later chapters are concerned with the human panic and disruption caused by the Martians' arrival.
6. These descriptions of panic are not just put in for the sake of horror, since Wells is concerned with the nature of human civilisation and the speed with which it could be destroyed.
7. C. S. Lewis gives a perceptive but one-sided view of *The War of the Worlds*. Wells's subject is not only the nature of extra-terrestrial beings, but of Man—'civilised', nineteenth-century Man—himself.

Specimen questions

Comprehension

Read the following passage carefully, and then answer each of the questions about it:

> I remained a very long time upon the roof, wondering at the grotesque changes of the day. I recalled my mental states from the midnight prayer to the foolish card-playing. I had a violent revulsion of feeling. I remember I flung away the cigar with *a certain wasteful symbolism*. My folly came to me with glaring exaggeration. I seemed *a traitor to my wife and to my kind*; I was filled with remorse. I resolved to leave this strange undisciplined dreamer of great things to his drink and gluttony, and to go on into London. There, it seemed to me, I had the best chance of learning what the Martians and my fellow-men were doing. I was still upon the roof when the late moon rose.

(i) At what point in the story did the narrator stay upon the roof as described here?
(ii) What were the 'grotesque changes of the day' that he recalled?
(iii) Explain the meaning of each of the phrases here printed in italics.
(iv) Who was the 'strange undisciplined dreamer of great things'?
　　Comment on the appropriateness of this summary of his character.
(v) What were the 'Martians and my fellow-men' doing at this time?

Synopsis

(i) Write a brief history of the Martian invasion of the Earth.
(ii) Describe the narrator's adventures after he escaped from his imprisonment in the ruined house.

Critical and thematic

(i) To what extent does *The War of the Worlds* illustrate the Victorian idea of 'Nature red in tooth and claw'?
(ii) Analyse the use made of contemporary scientific theories in *The War of the Worlds*.
(iii) 'Although *The War of the Worlds* employs the methods of minute documentary realism, it tells a story of universal significance.' Discuss.
(iv) 'In *The War of the Worlds*, Wells is able to make the reader see the Martian as well as the human view of the conflict.' Discuss.
(v) It has been suggested that the aim of all science fiction is to arouse the 'sense of wonder'. How successful do you think Wells is in achieving this?

Part 5
Suggestions for further reading

WELLS, H. G.: *Experiment in Autobiography*, (2 vols), Gollancz and Cresset Press, London, 1934. Wells's own highly readable account of his life and thought.

PARRINDER, PATRICK: *H. G. Wells*, Capricorn Books, New York, 1977. A wide-ranging introductory study of Wells's achievement as a novelist, with a full bibliography.

BERGONZI, BERNARD: *The Early H. G. Wells*, Manchester University Press, Manchester, 1961. The most influential study of Wells's 'scientific romances', with an excellent chapter on *The War of the Worlds*.

CLARKE, I. F.: *Voices Prophesying War 1763–1984*, Oxford University Press, Oxford, 1966. Discusses *The War of the Worlds* in the context of other 'future war' stories of the late nineteenth century.

MACKENZIE, NORMAN AND JEANNE: *The Time Traveller: The Life of H. G. Wells*, Weidenfeld and Nicolson, London, 1973. The standard modern account of Wells's life and times.

ROSE, MARK (ED.): *Science Fiction: A Collection of Critical Essays*, Prentice-Hall, Englewood Cliffs, N.J., 1976. Essays on science fiction by a variety of critics, with important contributions by C. S. Lewis, Susan Sontag and Darko Suvin.

The author of these notes

PATRICK PARRINDER was educated at the University of Cambridge. He was a Fellow of King's College, Cambridge, and an Assistant Lecturer at the University of Cambridge before taking up his present post at the University of Reading, where he is a Reader in English. He has published *H. G. Wells* (1970) in the Writers and Critics Series; *H. G. Wells: The Critical Heritage* (1972); *Authors and Authority* (1977); and is editor of *Science Fiction: A Critical Guide* (1979). He has also contributed articles and reviews to various journals.